More Advance Praise for *Targeted*

"Part history and part handbook, *Targeted* is an inside look at the way digital advertising impacts both businesses and consumers. Mike Smith offers a thoughtful, in-depth study of how online advertising is delivered now, and how it will be in the future."

—PAUL SCIARRA, *Cofounder, Pinterest*

"*Targeted* is a must-read for anyone interested in the digital business today. Learn how to target your customers by reading one of the most detailed and informative books on the topic. Smith knows the "ins and outs" of this complicated medium and draws on his decades of experience from HBO to Forbes to Hearst. This book is a good read for industry veterans as well as the general consumer who wants to know more about why particular ads appear every time they log in to their computer or mobile device."

—DAVE MOORE, *Chairman, Xaxis, and President, WPP Digital*

"Technology has been the driving force of Mike Smith's career. Now he has chosen to share his knowledge of digital advertising to educate and enlighten those in the industry, as well as entrepreneurs, business executives, educators, and even consumers. The internet and digital advertising are here to stay. It's time to learn what is happening behind computer screens and mobile devices and discover how to take advantage of the knowledge Smith shares."

—DR. JOEL BLOOM, *Pres...   ...gy*

"The world of digital advertising offers many, many advances for marketers of all shapes and sizes…but it also has some very big negatives. It can seem incredibly complex and that complexity can help foster unethical and at times illegal activities on unsuspecting advertisers. Mr. Smith understands this digital ecosystem and gives an inside look at not only the realities of today's marketplace but how we got here as well. He offers insight into how to make the most of the staggering marketing opportunities that are available today while staying clear of the most destructive black–hat activities. This book is a must–read for newcomers and established online marketers alike."

—JIM SPANFELLER, *Founder and CEO, TheDailyMeal.com and TheActiveTimes.com*

"Mike Smith takes you on an informative journey through the history of online advertising—covering the technology, data and players responsible for the incredible innovation that has taken place in the past two decades—and provides a view into the future of addressable advertising. Ad execs, business owners, online information seekers and savvy shoppers must read *Targeted*." —DENISE COLELLA, *CEO, Maxifier*

"I am a product–driven CEO running a technology company. I know that engineering a solution that intersects with the needs of the customer and a rapidly evolving marketplace can be a difficult task. I rely on the digital media executives as a reference point to achieve this. Within that community, Mike Smith is among the most progressive and innovative thought leaders on the sell side of the market. Not content to sit on the sidelines and wait for the popular choice, he is leading the industry forward and defining the standard along the way. *Targeted* is a must–read for all media professionals, entry–level to C–suite. It is an end–to–end look at the fascinating and dynamic digital media market, written by one of the most relevant digital media executives in the space." —MICHAEL CONNELLY, *CEO, Sonobi*

Targeted

Targeted

*How Technology Is Revolutionizing Advertising
and the Way Companies Reach Consumers*

Mike Smith

△AMACOM

American Management Association

New York • Atlanta • Brussels • Chicago • Mexico City • San Francisco
Shanghai • Tokyo • Toronto • Washington, D.C.

Bulk discounts available. For details visit:
www.amacombooks.org/go/specialsales
Or contact special sales:
Phone: 800–250–5308
Email: specialsls@amanet.org
View all the AMACOM titles at: www.amacombooks.org
American Management Association: www.amanet.org

This publication is designed to provide accurate and authoritative information in regard to the subject matter covered. It is sold with the understanding that the publisher is not engaged in rendering legal, accounting, or other professional service. If legal advice or other expert assistance is required, the services of a competent professional person should be sought.

Library of Congress Cataloging-in-Publication Data

Smith, Mike, 1966–
  Targeted : how technology is revolutionizing advertising and the way companies reach consumers / Mike Smith.
    pages cm
  Includes index.
  ISBN 978-0-8144-3499-4 (hardcover) — ISBN 0-8144-3499-1 (hardcover) — ISBN 978-0-8144-4901-1 (ebook) 1. Internet advertising. 2. Internet marketing. 3. Target marketing. I. Title.
  HF6146.I58S65 2015
  659.1'11–dc23   2014021250

About AMA

American Management Association (www.amanet.org) is a world leader in talent development, advancing the skills of individuals to drive business success. Our mission is to support the goals of individuals and organizations through a complete range of products and services, including classroom and virtual seminars, webcasts, webinars, podcasts, conferences, corporate and government solutions, business books, and research. AMA's approach to improving performance combines experiential learning—learning through doing—with opportunities for ongoing professional growth at every step of one's career journey.

Printing number

10 9 8 7 6 5 4 3 2 1

I dedicate this book to my supportive and loving wife, Denise,
and to our wonderful children, Jessica and Michael.
My family's belief in me enables me to feel I can do anything.

To my late parents, Edward and Patricia Smith,
who continue to inspire me.

And to my amazing mother-in-law, Darlene Manfra,
with deep fondness and appreciation.

Contents

Acknowledgments

All authors incur debts and wish to thank those who have helped them in the production of their books. As a first-time author, I'm different in only one respect. My debts are so numerous and so deep that incurring them has been one of the most gratifying experiences of my life. So many people helped me so generously and tirelessly that this book became better than I ever could have produced on my own. The result of around four hundred interviews with the outstanding people mentioned here, this book has been elevated by *their* contributions into something beyond what I had hoped for when I started the project.

Before I acknowledge any others, I want to express my heartfelt appreciation for my partner on this book, Steven Flax. An award-winning business journalist, editor in chief, and experienced editorial project manager, Steve has made this collaboration one of the brightest spots of my professional life. Steve has brought a deep understanding of advertising technology, a businessman's perspective, creativity, and, not incidentally, an enormous number of insightful sources to this project. Working with him has been a continual pleasure, and I will miss our daily conversations.

Collectively, the innovators and entrepreneurs who have built advertising technology into the fascinating, disruptive, and creative industry that it is have come to personify to me the restless innovation, determination, and resilience that is human nature at its best. How high is the pedestal that these people deserve? The most high. My naming and thanking them individually here is one of the happiest aspects of becoming an author.

Brian O'Kelley, Dave Morgan, Bill Wise, Matt Philips, Michael Walrath, John Donahue, Jonah Goodhart, Noah Goodhart, Tim Cadogan, Ted Meisel, Bill Gross, Eric Picard, Scott Kurnit, Mike Baker, Bill Simmons, Michael Rubenstein, Chris Stevens, Jim Spanfeller, John Taysom, Bill Demas, Phil Smolin, Suman Chagarlamudi, Joe Zawadzki, Ari Buchalter, Mark Mannino, Matthew Goldstein, Tom Chavez, Roger McNamee, Ted Shergalis, Dr. PJ Gurumohan, Rajeev Goel, Nat Turner, Mark Zagorski, Edward Montes, Jeff Green, Mike Seiman, Russ Fradin, Omar Tawakol, Zach Coelius, Ramsey McGrory, Terence Kawaja, Niel Robertson, David Moore, Aaron Letscher, Edward Kozek, Kevin Lee, Joe Doran, Josh Shatkin-Margolis, Michael Cassidy, Gil Beyda, Adam Lehman, Kevin O'Connor, Wenda Harris Millard, Dr. Deb Roy, Philipp Pieper, and Dr. Skip Brand.

Lori Ames for her guidance throughout this project and for helping me with publicity, marketing, and public relations. I am grateful to Dana Newman, my literary agent, for her expert guidance. I am also grateful to the team at my publisher, AMACOM Books: Ellen Kadin, Barry Richardson, Andy Ambraziejus, Erika Spelman, and Kama Timbrell, and the team at North Market Street Graphics: Ginny Carroll, Cindy Szili, and Mike Dunnick.

Denise Smith, Jessica Smith, and Michael Smith II.

I have the good fortune of working at Hearst Corporation and would like to thank my colleagues for their support on this project: David Carey, Troy Young, Phil Wiser, Lincoln Millstein, Steven R. Swartz, Mark Aldam, Neeraj Khemlani, Alexandra Carlin, Debi Chirichella, Todd Haskell, Michael Clinton, Gabrielle Munoz Klass, John Weisgerber, Michael Benham, Heather

Keltz, Jessica Hoy, Jessica Mason, Brooke Edwards, Scott Both, James Jackson, Weyland Jung, Jacqueline Bertozzi, Susan Parker, Dave Morin, Ali Abelson, Brittany Cerbie, Jenny Erasmus, Grant Whitmore, and Sara Badler.

The Forbes family has been very kind to me since I began to work at *Forbes* in January 2000. I would like to express my gratitude to Tim Forbes, Steve Forbes, Bob Forbes, Kip Forbes, Wally Forbes, Moira Forbes, and Miguel Forbes.

Mike Perlis, Michael Federle, Kevin Gentzel, Michael Dugan, Steve Bond, Lewis D'Vorkin, Andrea Spiegel, Scott Masterson, Bill Flatley, Paul Maidment, Maureen Farrell, Bruce Rogers, Kai Falkenberg, Suren Ter-Saakov, Achir Kalra, Alyson Papalia, Elizabeth Sobel, Christopher LaBianca, Meredith Levien, Mark Howard, Stephanie Mazzamaro, Mia Carbonell, Lauren Gurnee, Sharon Jautz, Mark Binger, Dan Papalia, Rebeca Solorzano, and Andrew Cassin.

Beth Wallace, Paul Martino, Darius Daftary, Mike Yavonditte, James Altucher, Ari Bluman, Albie Collins, Jim Flock, Steve Morgan, Grant Whitmore, Kevin English, Gerard Baglieri, Sharon Gitelle, and John French.

David Hallerman, Stephanie Flosi, Andrew Lipsman, Dan Marcec, Shira Orbach, Sherrill Mane, Kristina Sruoginis, Elizabeth Luke, Namit Merchant, Chevan Nanayakkara, Katrin Magnusson, David Rosenblatt, Dave Simon, Maureen Little, Paul Alfieri, Jonathan Gardner, Leslie Lee, Shane Keats, Denise Vardakas-Styrna, Marc Rotenberg, Jules Polonetsky, Alan Chapell, J. Trevor Hughes, Professor Noah Feldman, Richard Sobel, Professor Rosabeth Moss Kanter, Dr. David Cleevely, Dr. Latanya Sweeney, Professor Sherry Turkle, Professor Lawrence Lessig, Professor Gabriel Kahn, Professor Paul Glimcher, and Professor Jim Waldo.

S. Ashlie Beringer, Jeff Jonas, Don Epperson, Jessica Breault (and her sweet new son, Mason), Jason Young, Jo Bowman, Meghan Brown, Kevin Lyons, Dave Tice, Jordan Elpern-Waxman, Rodney Mayers, Brad Terrell, Andy Ellenthal, Susan Marshall, Jonathan Greenglass, Ewa Dominowska, Ari Rosenberg, Joe Mandese, Risa Wexler, and John Gray.

Pat Dignan, Vincent Paolozzi, Marc Parrish, and Dave Martin.

Targeted

Introduction

The Internet is a compelling engine of engagement. It's a network where we can get any kind of information, conduct our business, and connect with others anywhere in the world at any time. This relentlessly churning and navigable Amazon of information and interaction has channels numbering in the millions through which the current flows in any direction. No medium ever invented gives us so much control over our entrances and exits. We can leave it on a whim and without any effort. It is changing our lives in ways we need to pay attention to. Its influence is and will be as profound as if something had been implanted in our brains or had modified our genome.

Everything we get from the Internet we get for free because others pay for it.[1] The Internet has grown and been sustained by advertising. Whether we think publishers have earned our attention or advertisers have hijacked it, it is money from advertising that has put the content at our disposal. Advertisers subsidize the medium to get our attention, however fleeting or ungovernable it may be, in order to pitch their products to us.

To some, this phenomenon is like a beanstalk on Internet growth hormone, which will lead to a bonanza in cyberspace. To others, it's the humongous man-eating plant from *Little Shop of Horrors*, insidiously tracking them and invading their privacy.

However you see it, there is no denying that digital advertising in all its forms is vastly different from every sort of advertising that has preceded it. It has grown and transformed itself with stunning speed. As with the Internet that spawned it, it is changing the future we will inhabit. Even as "realists" assumed digital advertising was a gimmick with little utility, it went from a concept in entrepreneurs' imaginations and the wishful thinking of venture capitalists to an apparatus of commercial promotion that reached critical mass while many were still wondering if it was for real.

As an executive in digital publishing since January 2000—for thirteen years at my former employer, Forbes Media LLC, and, now, at Hearst Corporation—I can testify that the trajectory of digital advertising has been rocketlike. From a standing start, the market for digital advertising became substantial in less than twenty years. In 2013, in the United States alone, advertisers spent $42.8 billion[2] for digital advertising—approximately one of every four dollars spent for advertising of any kind.[3] Those $42.8 billion 2013 digital ad revenues amount to approximately $11.4 billion more than the print advertising revenues of newspapers and magazines *combined*. It's 57 percent of what was spent on TV advertising ($74.5 billion), the biggest single advertising medium.[4] Back in 2011, digital advertising surpassed what was spent for cable TV. Perhaps most noteworthy, in 2013, digital advertising exceeded what was spent for broadcast TV. The two forms of TV advertising *combined* may still be greater than digital advertising, but digital advertising is now bigger than either type of TV media individually.[5] PricewaterhouseCoopers predicts that by 2017 the worldwide market for digital advertising will reach $185 billion.[6]

That's a big claim, but it's not only for advertising that you see on your computer; it also includes advertising that you see on *any* networked device, such as your tablet, mobile phone, and TV (or any other device showing video, such as an iPod Touch). It encompasses whatever advertising and sponsored links you encounter when you do a search or use social media such as Facebook or Twitter. According to a June 2014 forecast by eMarketer, by 2017 total U.S. digital advertising revenues will reach $74.1 billion, almost equal to what will be spent on TV advertising ($75.98 billion), and advertising on mobile devices ($47.4 billion) will be the fastest-growing share of the digital ad total.[7] As projected by eMarketer, by 2018, digital media's share of total annual U.S. ad spending will surpass that of TV, broadcast plus cable (a 37.3 percent share for all digital media vs. a 35.7 percent share for all forms of TV combined).[8]

But online advertising is unprecedented for much more than its current size and its recent growth. It's also exceptional because the Internet is drastically different from any other medium of communications that advertisers have used. Among its many distinctions, it has spawned an exponential proliferation of publishers, it has liberated viewers from fixed schedules for getting content, and it has empowered its audience in ways that traditional media never has.

While the audience for digital content is enormous and global, it is also ultrafragmented. It can be composed of the tiniest slivers of audience groups. Never has an audience of this aggregate size been this disaggregated. This is an audience that can consist, at times, of cohorts of one. Today, if a wealthy shopper somewhere on the Internet is in the market for an expensive luxury car *right now*, targeting that one shopper at that moment may be more valuable than advertising to millions of unmotivated consumers, who, two generations ago, were watching *I Love Lucy* at the same time and may have been wondering if they had time to go to the bathroom during the commercial break.

Viewers who browse the Internet are much more independent than past consumers of mass media. They can instantaneously leave the web page where your ad appears with unprecedented ease and lack of loyalty. Clicking on links, they can go wherever they want whenever they want. They are capable of verging-on-anarchic nonallegiance.

But if this audience has unprecedented ease in getting out of your corral, it is also capable of being incredibly responsive to your message. You can tap into that responsiveness because every individual in this audience is trackable and addressable. That is vastly valuable to advertisers. Online advertising to this audience is a two-way street. Audience members are able to react to your ad in real time, providing feedback that was unavailable to traditional mass media years ago. The Internet connection is bidirectional. Because of the real-time analytics that can be associated with an online ad, a savvy, Internet-sophisticated advertiser can learn, in the moment, who is watching and engaging with the ad, where they live, what their household income is, if and how they share their experiences by means of social media, as well as other commercially useful data. This is not just a matter of the *cookies* that worry privacy advocates so much. It is also enabled by the Internet Protocol (IP) address for whatever networked device—computer, tablet, mobile phone, Internet TV, or whatever else may be invented—they are using to get the information. Even microwave ovens and refrigerators can have IP addresses. At the moment the viewer responds to an ad or a sweepstakes, or delves more deeply into an item of interest, he or she may be generating a geyser of data that advertisers can learn from.

But if the opportunities are great for Internet advertising, so are the challenges. For starters, three out of four dollars spent on advertising in the United States are spent on other competing ad media. Some in advertising still see digital advertising as the tail, not the dog. Creating online advertising is not seen by ad agency creatives and account executives as cool, sexy, and exciting work from which big bucks can be made.

In addition, Internet publishing poses a number of challenges generated by the technology that created it. The number of websites and web publishers proliferates rapidly because it's so easy to publish online content, which creates the opportunity for presenting zillions of ads. Web publishing has the capability to generate so many ads (or, more accurately, the spaces where the ads could go on the web page, which are called *im-*

pressions) that the supply seems to be verging on infinite. The huge supply commoditizes web ads, holding down prices.

Moreover, presenting those ads where and when they are supposed to appear (*ad serving*) becomes a big technological challenge. Unlike a big old billboard beside a highway with lots of traffic, online publishing is a communications channel in which the medium itself has a great many moving parts.

One group of moving parts is the *bots, web crawlers,* or *spiders* from search engines. For example, search engines send these automated cyber-critters crawling through content sites to log the appearance of search terms.[9] That's a legitimate aspect of the search function, but advertisers should not be charged for such robotic, nonhuman activity at a site. They should pay for only the people who might view their ad, so those who sell online media have to filter these virtual viewers out of their site census. Publishers have the responsibility to remove such nonhuman traffic from the audience accounting.

There is another effect of the potentially vast supply of ads: clutter. The glut of cyberclutter makes it more difficult for premium sites and their premium impressions to stand out. With vast numbers of pages devoted daily to reporting on Lindsay Lohan's nightlife, sites with better content can be appreciated for being better and special only if they can gain enough attention for their quality. That has gotten much harder.

For these reasons and for others that I'll go into in more detail, online advertising has the potential to be a powerful engine of impact. But, despite the technological wizardry it has already exhibited, it's still an engine without an automatic transmission. Sometimes the gears don't mesh well, and sometimes the ad serving isn't foolproof.

At times, that has led to situations in which advertisers' ads did not appear when or where they were supposed to. A Fidelity ad may be very effective when it appears before extremely wealthy investors when they are browsing the Forbes.com site and have their portfolios in mind. The same ad shown to the same viewers may be much less effective if it's shown to them when they're viewing sites devoted to their recreational interests or to social media.

There have also been cases in which advertisers were overcharged because the number of viewers who supposedly saw their ads was over-estimated, sometimes deliberately (called *click fraud*). Compared to traditional advertising in print or on TV, fraud in online advertising is more easily concealed. Because the technology beneath the web page is so complex, the medium is much more opaque. It's a black box. It would take a really good hacker-engineer to determine if a site tended to overstate the viewer traffic that it reported. It's not as simple as counting cattle as they go through a chute.

As the market for online advertising has developed, it poses its own special deal-making difficulties. On May 3, 2010, Terence Kawaja, the CEO of LUMA Partners LLC, a boutique mergers-and-acquisitions consulting firm, gave the keynote speech at the Networks and Exchanges meeting of the Interactive Advertising Bureau (IAB). The speech was titled "Parsing the Mayhem." Figure I-1, with Kawaja's permission, shows a recently updated version of the third slide from his talk.

Does this slide illustrate a free, fair, transparent, and efficient market?

It might not be fair for me to say. As executives at Hearst, which is a publisher, my colleagues and I are players and principals in the market. We're, perhaps, too close to the situation. Suffice it to say that when Kawaja gave his speech and showed the slide, which went viral throughout the online ad industry, the market for online advertising was far from an advanced economic life-form. In contrast to thriving habitats, in new business markets sometimes you can have too much biodiversity. For example, in the United States online advertising business, one category of intermediaries—ad networks—numbered more than 350 companies when Kawaja gave his speech.

The industry has so many players poised between the publishers and advertisers that it can sometimes feel like a stock exchange in which every company's stock has its own market maker. This does not lend itself to easy

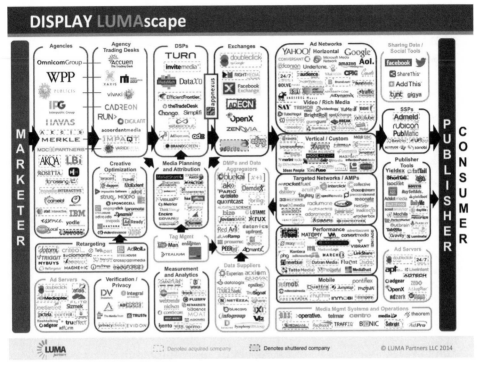

FIGURE I-1　*Display advertising technology landscape (Source: LUMA Partners)*

comparison shopping or prudent deal making. That's a bit of an exagger-ation, but Ramsey McGrory, formerly head of Right Media, an ad network that operates an online exchange, has said of Kawaja's slide, "It's a pain-fully complex map." When McGrory came to Forbes in December 2010 to give a talk to the ad ops (advertising operations) staff, his advice, which he gave all the time to Right Media's employees, was "Embrace the murkiness."

There is a lot of murkiness to embrace. Clearly, the industry has a long way to go to become a fair, free, and efficient market. Now around 78 percent of ad sales take place between publishers and advertisers (with some intermediaries) and not on online exchanges. By conducting business this way, each party must use its subjective judgment about how much a certain viewer seeing an ad in a certain place at a certain time is worth. Wherever there is subjective judgment, there inevitably is wishful thinking or the enforcement of market advantage. In a buyers' market, it's the buyers' appraisal of value that prevails. Sellers may disagree; nevertheless, they tend to concede the point. That's not evidence of the correctness of the bid as an estimation of value.

A Look Back and to the Future

In *Targeted*, we examine some of the highlights of the development of digital advertising over the past twenty event-filled years. Because the question "How do you value an ad?" is so important, we put special emphasis on the technologies that have helped the business advance in that regard.

Perhaps the most noteworthy of those technological innovations has been *real-time bidding* (RTB) on online ad exchanges. Transactions on such exchanges represent only a little more than 20 percent of digital display ad sales. But such transactions, made in fractions of a second using real-time bidding technologies, have the capability to establish value in a way that strips away much of the intuition and subjectivity. RTB also has a bias toward fairness. The deal is clinched by the bidder who is willing to pay the most.

In real-time bidding on ad exchanges, there comes a moment, a millisecond, when a prudent (for the buyer) and advantageous (for the seller) real-dollar value is placed on a fleeting impression on an Internet page. Whatever is the opposite of just "kicking the tires," that's what is going on in RTB. It is happening billions of times every day. At present, such RTB may give values for our impressions that we publishers might regard as undeservedly low. Nevertheless, I am in awe of the technological ingenuity our industry has displayed.

My goal in this book is to explain clearly how powerfully enabling technologies such as paid-search advertising and real-time bidding work. In addition, I want to take you behind the scenes to describe how some of the industry's most brilliant innovators developed such technologies and created the novel business models of some of the outstanding companies that serve the future of digital ad sales.

I have been fascinated and, at times, a little whiplashed by being a part of this fast-developing field and seeing at least some of it from behind the scenes. In many ways it mirrors what is happening on a far broader scale in society as a whole.

One of the lessons I have learned is that even if you have the latest, greatest technology or the cleverest, most advantageous business model, sometimes neither of those is enough to ensure success. Sometimes neither—nor both—is sufficient. Even with such assets, the distinguishing factors in success are often management skill, flexibility, and the initiative that only leadership can elicit. No matter how powerful or capable the new technology is, it's such human factors that make the difference. That's why, even though *Targeted* emphasizes the technologies that have helped digital advertising to advance, I take heart from the crucial role we all play in making our enterprises work.

The advertising industry has grown enormously. It has also made great strides in developing fairness and efficiency. Five years ago it was way murkier than it is now. I hope that, by featuring prominently many of the technological innovations and their creators who have advanced this industry, I will help you better understand, manage, and promote the future of this dynamic business.

CHAPTER 1

The Congested Online Ecosystem

The development of online advertising has been characterized by rapid growth, ingenious technological innovation, and restless entrepreneurialism that have spawned the proliferation of competing business models. But, novel technology and entrepreneurial initiative aside, the essence of the business, as with any other advertising medium, is to present a compellingly effective ad to the right person at the right time and place for a price that makes sense to the seller and potential buyer. For the principals, the advertisers and publishers, as Sam sang in *Casablanca*, "the fundamental things apply."

Yet optimizing those fundamentals for a radically new digital medium has proved very complex. While, in less than twenty years, online advertising has become a substantial share of all advertising in the United States, its growth has been more like an uphill battle than a superhighway, at least when it comes to making money. Why?

One reason is that it's "same old, same old." That is, it's advertising.

Some of the other reasons are that it's new and different. It's digital, dynamic, and interactive. First, let's look at the same old, same old.

Everyone knows that advertising works. We have all been persuaded by an ad to buy something we hadn't intended to buy. On the other hand, we all know that plenty of advertising doesn't work. All of us have ignored ads. Furthermore, we have often seen ads for which we knew we were not the appropriate audience. So all of us have experienced the futility and wastefulness of advertising. This will be true when online advertising becomes as prehistoric as a Paleolithic flint knife.

Then, too, at times it's hard to demonstrate the causal connection between advertising and the awareness or purchase of the products the ads are supposed to promote.

Because of this acknowledged wastefulness, and because the efficacy of advertising has sometimes been more apparent than proven, during adverse economic times, ad spending customarily finds itself in the crosshairs of companies' cost cutters. Often, it's the first category of spending to go to the corporate guillotine. In the bloodless jargon of the management consultant, it's a "discretionary expense."

Now let's turn to those other reasons—what could be called "the penalty of novelty." Online advertising, for a number of years, was something of a stepchild among ad media just because it was so new and different. Early in the Internet era, the content found on websites was derivative and pedestrian, just cut-and-pasted pages from print publications—often disparagingly called "shovelware." The user experience in the early days of Internet browsing was dismally similar to that of the early days of cable TV. Moreover, without such highlights of cable advertising as the Ginsu knife,[1] the ad content of early websites was also pretty lackluster.

These obstacles were compounded by the inertia inherent in a new advertising channel up for adoption. Ad sales were few, as were viewers. It was all so *new*. Career advertising agency executives didn't understand the new medium. There was a well-entrenched, media-buying infrastructure that was unfamiliar with online advertising. In many agencies, let's just say that developing online ads was not a great career move.

The online medium was also plagued by confusion about *what to measure* and *who should do it* (later chapters discuss competing metrics in greater detail). Should the effectiveness of the medium be measured by the number of unique viewers at a site, by clicks, by leads, or by acquisitions, among other measures? The technological ingenuity of the online channel had led to a proliferation of competing, clamoring metrics. Their Ginsu ingenuity notwithstanding, there was no consensus metric of ad performance—something that tends to thwart ad spending. By contrast, with TV advertising, as Terry Kawaja points out, "No one argues about the value of a Nielsen rating point."

The online channel has also been beset by certain inherent vagaries. Users can come to a site from anywhere at any time. Moreover, with online media, the existence of the ad space, or the impression, happens on the spur of the moment. Only as a web page is being rendered for each new user does the ad space come into being. This creation of the ad space in the moment is the opposite of the static and enduring placement of a billboard.

Ad spending follows eyeballs. It's just as true online. So welcome to our site, right? Yet, on Internet sites, those eyeballs are mystifyingly hard to keep in sight. Their attendance at a given site could be so brief, and they could leave with such suddenness. The event can be so fleeting, it is like trying to advertise to the dew as it's evaporating.

During the early part of the previous decade, traditional ad agencies were still trying to match brands with the ever-increasing number of sites on the Internet. Since then, the terrain of interactive advertising has experienced tectonic shifts with the rise of paid-search advertising, advertising networks, and real-time bidding, along with the advent of social media and the proliferation of tablets and smartphones. But the gap between advertisers and online publishers remained, with the former trying to figure out how to target consumers with increasing accuracy and the latter at a loss about what to do with the sudden glut of unsold inventory—that is, the white space that may appear on your browser's screen.[2]

As the number of sites online proliferated, and audiences fragmented into narrower and narrower niches, ad agencies found they lacked the relationships and resources to adroitly use the exponentially expanding resources of online publishers. Advertisers also had little experience allocating budgets across so many potential spaces. Furthermore, brands and agencies were suddenly expected to deliver proof of consumer engagement against a new set of online metrics and return-on-investment (ROI) benchmarks.

In addition, in its early days, ad serving on the Internet was fraught with technical difficulties as well as difficulties in determining optimization and fulfillment. *Optimization* here means getting the most impact from an ad or from some amount of spending for ad media. *Fulfillment* means the ad was shown to the potential consumer to whom the advertiser wanted to show it. Publishers in the new medium (including established major print publishers who were trying to become online moguls) often lacked the resources to fill their ad space. They simply didn't have the ad sales staff and account management teams sufficiently knowledgeable in the new medium to help advertisers optimize their branding campaigns. Developing those relationships required a depth of management, expertise, and time that online publishers often lacked.

Deals Along the Internet Highway

A number of new, technologically savvy start-ups—new types of intermediaries—arose to make different aspects of ad serving work better for different types of clients, whether publishers or advertisers. Someone had to find a way to help both advertisers and publishers navigate the virtual topology of the Web world. These smaller, agile start-ups, staffed by people who had gained expertise in various subsegments of the markets, had experience making use of online data that neither advertisers nor publishers had developed in-house.

The great promise of interactive advertising, after all, was improved accuracy, targeting, effectiveness, and transparency. The amount of data suddenly available about consumer behavior and preferences promised to make the Nielsen TV rating system seem antiquated.

A range of new media partners entered the digital field to give guidance to both the brand-marketing and publishing sides. These intermediaries proposed to help advertisers optimize their placements and publishers sell their inventory, thereby bridging the online marketing gap.

To understand the opportunity for and the behavior of these intermediaries, it helps to take a closer look at your typical trip online.

The Toll Road

Imagine each time you go online as a trip to a new destination. The address of the web page that you type into the browser address field sets your desired endpoint, and the instant you hit the Return key, you're off. From your standpoint, the journey takes no longer than a few seconds. You take a sip of coffee, stare out the window, and, *voilà!*, your page is fully loaded and ready to read, almost as if by magic.

Inside the workings of the Internet, however, the route that brought you to, for example, *Esquire*'s homepage had many more stops than you might have realized. Let's think of those stops as tollbooths. Standing between you looking at a blank browser screen and you arriving at your ultimate destination—the fully loaded web page you selected—are a horde of invisible toll collectors (the intermediaries), each of which collects a small cut of every advertising dollar so that you can visit the page you picked.

These tollbooth operators are those firms that play a role in ad serving, that help ensure that an ad gets to the right place on the page you intend to visit. Each receives a small piece of the money that was paid by the advertiser to place the ad on the appropriate page. All of the tollbooth operators, including, finally, the publisher of the web page, share in the revenues paid by the advertisers. In that way, they help keep the system running, and, as they do, small amounts of change (the tolls) add up to lots of dollars as thousands of viewers like you pass through their tollbooths.

How much do all those online tolls amount to? According to one widely accepted analysis,[3] for every $5 an advertiser pays to place an ad online to be viewed by one thousand suitable consumers (called the *cost per thousand*, or CPM), the publisher on whose web pages the ads appear customarily gets less than $2. (We'll come back in a later chapter to the enormous cost imposed by intermediaries, when we discuss alternatives to the toll road I have just described.)

Let's imagine a site published by Hearst—say, www.esquire.com—as the end of the highway. That's your objective. At the other end are the advertisers who, in a sense, are sponsoring your journey to that destination. Nowadays, an almost dizzyingly complex conglomeration of entities falls somewhere in the middle, between you and that destination.

Making up this complicated chain of intermediaries is some combination or all of the following: demand- and supply-side platforms, data optimizers and providers, ad exchanges, and ad networks, among others. And each of these many parties gets some sliver of the payment between the brand marketer and Hearst, as they enable you to get the content that you want.

To better understand the invisible mechanisms that deliver the Internet to your screen, let's take a look at some of the principal service providers ("toll collectors"; see Figure 1-1).

The Toll Collectors

PUBLISHERS: If you have followed the news even casually over the last few years, it's likely that you came across a story about publishing in crisis. (In fact, you probably saw that story on a screen instead of reading it on paper.) While rumors of newspapers' last gasps have been greatly exagger-

FIGURE 1-1
The highway and the toll collectors

ated, no one in any part of the media food chain would deny the industry upheaval that is reshaping the publishing world.

For our purposes, a publisher is any content provider whose business model is providing information that is paid for by advertising. This includes portals like AOL, MSN, and Yahoo!; traditional news and special interest outlets such as nytimes.com, cnn.com, and esquire.com; search engines such as Google and Bing; and social media sites like Facebook and LinkedIn. These publishers may be "platform agnostic." That is, they may deliver content by means of more than one medium. So, for example, Hearst provides *Esquire*'s content both in print and online.

AD NETWORKS: Now we're getting into the heavily trafficked part of the toll road, where the most transactions take place. As Internet use expanded, most ad agencies did not have adequate media-buying resources to select and purchase ad spaces (impressions) across the multitude of websites suddenly sprouting up. Ad networks arose to meet this need for selective and efficient ad space allocation for presenting what are called *display ads*, which look like little billboards. They bought ad space in bulk from publishers, often at prices far below the full retail prices publishers asked for. Often, the impressions they bought were those the publishers were unable to sell—or unable to sell for good prices (known as *remnant inventory*). Then the ad networks resold their aggregate inventory across the Internet to advertisers and their ad agencies. (See Chapter 5 for a more detailed account of this moment in interactive advertising history.)

Some of the noteworthy ad networks are AOL's Advertising.com, the Yahoo! Network, DoubleClick, Microsoft Media Network, and 24/7 Real Media. DoubleClick (which now operates a major online ad exchange) is owned by Google, providing the search giant with a perch at many locations along the toll road—as publisher, exchange, network, and advertiser. Smaller ad networks, such as Blogads, Deck Network, and Federated Media, help advertisers reach more specialized, niche audiences on sites that have limited ad inventory. By using these smaller networks, advertisers gain the benefit of knowing they are reaching a desirable, very selective segment of consumers.

AD EXCHANGES: The primary function of an exchange is to aggregate ad space (supply) from publishers and sell it via an auction, thereby matching the supply with the demand (the advertisers), theoretically with greater efficiency than if publishers and advertisers interacted one-to-one. Publishers might divide their inventory among, and advertisers may buy impressions from, multiple ad networks, operating as intermediaries. In contrast to all that dividing and allocating, the premise of an ad exchange, as with a stock exchange, is the consolidation of inventory so that these inventory-clearing, ad-serving transactions can take place with greater transparency and scale and at prices that work best for buyers and sellers.

This category of the toll landscape has seen a big consolidation over the past several years. The most prominent ad exchanges have been acquired by major online media conglomerates. Right Media was acquired by Yahoo! in April 2007 for $680 million. DoubleClick was purchased by Google in May 2007 for $3.1 billion. Microsoft bought ad exchange AdECN in August 2007 for an undisclosed amount.

DEMAND-SIDE PLATFORMS: As the road between publishers and advertisers became more crowded with intermediaries, advertisers and their ad agencies began looking for help navigating the increasingly complex terrain. So-called demand-side platforms (DSPs) were formed to work for and consult with the buyers of online advertising. They offered expert services helping advertisers select potential audience members across ad networks and exchanges by, for example, helping them pick the right media and/or actually buying the media on behalf of their clients, promising advertisers that they could greatly improve their ability to target and buy specific audiences. By aggregating demand by means of DSPs, ad agencies and media buyers can better manage their campaigns across a range of sites. DSPs such as MediaMath, DataXu, and Turn Inc. help improve the selectiveness of those who buy ad space.

SUPPLY-SIDE PLATFORMS: These are companies that work with and consult for the publishers, the sellers. Their role is to help publishers make the most money in selling their media; that's why they are sometimes called yield optimization companies.

Since mass-media advertising began, brands have sought assurance that their ads were being heard or seen by the right prospective customers at the right time. Yet, as we saw earlier, the fragmentation of Internet audiences, the vagaries of viewers' attention, and their flitting among sites have raised doubts about the ability of publishers or ad networks to deliver the right target at the right time. Supply–side platforms (SSPs) rose to the challenge with technologies that demonstrated to advertisers that they were reaching those they wanted to target. SSPs work on behalf of publishers to help them sell more impressions and/or sell them at higher prices. Prominent players in the field include Admeld (now owned by Google), PubMatic, and the Rubicon Project. Publishers often enlist their help when they want to maximize their revenues by selling remnant ad inventory.

DATA AGGREGATORS/PROVIDERS: The growing use of the Internet has created a deluge of digital information about you: the identity and address of your computer, the make and model of your car, the online and off-line destinations you visit, and myriad other facts about your preferences. Given the increased splintering of online audiences, behavioral data about who is doing what and when grows more valuable.

BlueKai, eXelate, Nielsen, Intelius, and Spokeo are some of the companies currently providing or mediating the exchange of data. Such data gathering is controversial because it arouses concerns that it infringes on our privacy. The increasing amassing of data files about individuals is met with suspicion, especially by consumer advocates, who view such data gathering as if it were a video camera keeping us all under surveillance. Nevertheless, it's likely that the growing volume of Internet traffic will only add to the amassing of data, especially as content is served in new ways by new networked devices (for example, tablet computers such as the iPad).

A Drive Down the Internet

Now that I have described some of the principal intermediaries between you and the website you want to visit, and sketched their business models and business interests, let's see how this actually plays out when you go online. Let's suppose you wanted to go to www.esquire.com, one of Hearst's sites. You'd type in the web address, hit return, and off you'd go. But while the address field on your web browser said one thing—

http://www.esquire.com—and stayed that way for as long as it took the page to load, the browser went through a great many tollbooths before reaching its destination.

Here's a list of the waypoints the browser visited—in a few thousandths of a second—while it was loading *Esquire's* homepage: ad.doubleclick.net (DoubleClick's ad server), p.raasnet.com (Hearst's core audience trading desk), pq-direct.revsci.net (AudienceScience, an ad tech platform), contextual.media .net (Media.net, a paid search syndication service), static.nrelate.com (nRelate, a content marketing firm), pubads.g.doubleclick.net (AdX, the Google online ad exchange), ads.pubmatic.com (site for PubMatic, an SSP), segment-pixel .invitemedia.com (DoubleClick's bid manager subsidiary, a DSP), loadm .exelator.com (site for eXelate, a third-party data provider), s.ixiaa.com (IXI, another third-party data provider), user.lucidmedia.com (site for Videology, an ad network for video), c.betrad.com (site for Evidon, a consumer privacy monitoring firm), beacon.walmart.com (site for Walmart, an advertiser), ce.lijit.com (site for Sovrn, a content marketing firm), r.nexac.com (site for Datalogix, a third-party data provider), d.adroll.com (site for AdRoll, an ad network), segments.adap.tv (site for Adap.TV, an ad network for video), and, finally, d.audienceiq.com (site for Outbrain, an audience analytics firm).

Eighteen stops before finally reading "Done." A trip with that many fast stops usually causes whiplash. Instead, the browser handled it all without blinking. Okay, maybe it blinked a few times. But from where you sat, the experience was pretty smooth and unruffled.

The data wizards working behind the scenes at each of these websites don't want you to pay any attention to what's going on back there. Frankly, you probably don't care anyway. You just want to see what's on the *Esquire* website. You have enough things on your mind without worrying about what byzantine set of queries your browser made so that the page could smoothly and quickly load and look right. But without this complex chain of handoffs from one profit-motivated digital traffic controller to the next, working behind the scenes, there would be infinitely less content than there is today. Without advertisers, there would be no *Esquire* website—or any other commercial website, for that matter—and much of the content on the Internet wouldn't exist. The reason there is so much content is that publishers provide it in order to make money. Without the economics and the technologies supporting the business, there wouldn't be much content to discover.

As I have just shown, this detour-filled road trip takes only seconds, or fractions of a second, depending on the speed of your browser. But what if it could be even faster? Even more efficient? With less money going to intermediaries? That's the promise of real-time bidding on ad exchanges. Chapter 6 goes into that in much more detail. But before we get to technologies for the sale of display ad impressions, it will help, first, to understand the development and use of paid-search advertising (Chapter 2), which was an indispensable predecessor of RTB.

CHAPTER 2

Search Engine Marketing

The ability to search at lightning speed through digital content is perhaps the most distinctive innovation that computers have put at users' and advertisers' fingertips. Paid-search advertising, an important part of search engine marketing (SEM), really is new and different. It's like harnessing a comet—one that lands almost in the instant it takes off, and there you are, with your ad, right at the comet's landing pad. Where search is concerned, computers are dazzling, and they make previous promotional media seem pretty dim and dawdling. As tireless, obedient, warp-speed search engines, computers behave like genies.

Here's how it works. Search engine advertisements are purchased from search engine companies like Google on the basis of keywords (that is, search terms or phrases, which may contain many words). There are two sorts of search engine marketing: search engine optimization (sometimes called "organic," "natural," or "SEO") and paid search.

In SEO, advertisers, agencies, and publishers hire specialists to optimize their content with the goal of winning high rankings on the search engine results pages (SERPs). In paid-search advertising, a paid-for ad or sponsored link appears near the occurrence of a search term on the SERP. For example, a maker of mountain bikes might pay a search engine company such as Google so that the bike maker's ad or a link to its website appears on the "mountain bike" SERP. Customarily, the bike company pays a certain amount only when someone viewing the SERP clicks on its ad or link. This pricing policy is called *pay per click* (PPC).

In addition to search advertising's amazing digital prestidigitation, it is important for a number of other reasons. First, it is an awesome traffic generator. According to a study by Borrell Associates, since 2009 five times as many people use search engines on a regular basis to find a local business than use the yellow pages.[1]

Furthermore, paid-search advertising, with its pay-per-click pricing policy, has settled some of the issues that have distressed advertisers. For example, there is little, if any, doubt that an ad has been seen—someone has to see the ad or link to click on it, right? In addition, PPC appears to satisfy advertisers' determination to pay for something only if it works. As Borrell Associates writes, "The magnetism of pay-per-click advertising is undeniable."[2]

Since 2003, paid-search advertising has outsold display advertising. A display ad (sometimes called a *banner ad*) is like a little billboard sitting on the web page. It is usually an illustration in a rectangle, box, or vertical column with some text. It can also be an interactive graphic that pops up or is animated somehow, or it can be a video that you turn on or that turns itself on. It's pictorial.

Paid search is the biggest segment of online advertising. Spending for paid-search advertising in the United States in 2013 was $19.9 billion, 46 percent of the digital advertising total, a new record. Spending for online display ads was $17.84 billion in 2013, around 42 percent of total U.S. online ad spend. An eMarketer forecast projects that annual paid-search ad spending will grow to $32.08 billion in the United States by 2018, a compound annual growth rate of 10.8 percent for the period 2012–2018.[3]

The Advantages of Paid Search

Display advertising has been around for ages, so why has a newcomer such as paid search been outselling it since 2003? For the same reason that cowboys wear spurs: because they work. Paid search is thought to be more like direct-response advertising than display is, and direct-response advertising is thought to work. Search advertisers believe that customers who see their ad soon after they have evidenced interest by searching for some topic will be more responsive. They regard seeing a display ad as a passive experience, often devoid of intent or even interest. "Audiences are more focused, engaged, and interested when doing searches," says David Hallerman, principal analyst at eMarketer.

Consumers often use a search engine to compare alternatives right before making a decision about what to buy. Paid-search ads can have a click-through rate (CTR) of around 10 percent, while display ads customarily get a CTR of one user out of every thousand (or less). A CTR of 0.1 percent is considered respectable for display advertising. That means that search users are one hundred times more likely to click on an ad than viewers of display ads. Such stats lead marketers to presume that Internet browsers using search are more likely to be in-market shoppers. Search advertisers are betting on—and paying for—search engine marketing's ability to drive immediate response and sales.

Search engine marketing also gets points because advertisers believe that it improves customer targeting. How? "Search engines [are] an easier way to figure out to whom to show your ad," says Suren Ter-Saakov, an authority on e-commerce, "because what users type in the search box expresses the user's interest in a clear, concrete form."

Perhaps most important, search engine marketing introduced the use of competitive bidding to determine placement—the ranking of advertisers—on the search engine results page. If you want your ad or link to be featured prominently, you can have it, if you're willing to pay for it. The highest bidder gets the link placed at the top of the stack on the SERP.

This was competitive bidding, *not* real-time bidding. It was, and still is, preconfigured bidding. It's an auction that happens *before* the search is conducted. The price is settled in advance. Nevertheless, paid-search advertising sold at auction served as an indispensable predecessor for the real-time auction exchanges—where bidding occurs in the moment—that have dramatically boosted the efficiency of selling display advertising on the Internet (see Chapters 6 and 7).

The introduction of auction selling, with its transparency, for which advertisers really have to thank GoTo.com, the predecessor of Overture Services, most compellingly raised the question: How much is it really worth to connect with a customer online? With the advent of auction selling, the process of putting a price on a click, and a value on search engine ads, went public. Online sales for paid-search advertising were now out in the open and subject to scrutiny, at least among interested and competitive bidders.

The Pitfalls of Paid Search

Paid-search advertising appears deceptively simple. Buy and link your ad to a keyword, then wait for customers to line up like zombies at a casting call for George Romero's *Night of the Living Dead*. However, it's one thing to bid on and buy a search term. It's another to conduct an effective paid-search ad campaign. Search advertisers have to pay as much attention to managing their campaigns as investors in companies whose shares trade on a stock exchange. There's a lot going on when the market is open, and the Internet never closes.

Picking the right keywords takes skill. You need to pick "steak branding iron," if you are selling little branding tools used to decorate steaks on your grill. If you choose the broader term "branding iron," you'll get lots of clicks (that you'll have to pay for) from ranchers, but probably no sales. There is a lot of wisdom in the slogan of Didit, a search marketing consulting firm in Mineola, New York: "Don't buy traffic; buy buyers."

As with Goldilocks, keywords can't be too narrow or too broad. They have to be just right. If they are not, there may be unintended consequences. For example, if you were selling replacement windows for buildings, it would be sensible to screen out keywords (to prevent associations you don't want) such as "software" and "program" to make sure that you don't get charged per click on every search that pertains to Microsoft's Windows operating system.

One search marketing services firm had as a client a law firm that served military personnel. The search services firm bought the keyword "Don't Ask, Don't Tell." When the term appeared a multitude of times in online media, paying for all those clicks became prohibitively expensive—too much of a good thing.[4]

Then there is geography to consider. If your window replacement business handles jobs only in the Poughkeepsie, New York, area, you have to restrict your keyword geographically by using the term "Poughkeepsie" if you don't want to start getting orders and paying for clicks from elsewhere.

Multiply this by the number of keywords that you have paid to link to, and you can see how complicated a keyword buy can be. Different keywords can cost different amounts at different times, can tap into different flows of traffic, and can incite users to click on them or respond to the ad at different rates. Each of these variables can also change in a moment or at different times of the day. The effectiveness of each can change, as can their return on investment, if your ad's placement rank goes up or down on the SERP.

What others are bidding can strongly affect where your link appears.

Here's an example that works to your advantage. If others stop bidding for your term of choice, you could rebid and get the term for less, and perhaps even elevate your rank on the SERP. That would improve your ROI—but only if you have been paying attention to the market and spotted the opportunity. Conversely, because competing advertisers are always changing their bids, your prominence on the SERP can fall if you are outbid. A high-ROI search term for which you were paying a reasonable price could suddenly become much less effective because your position on the SERP had deteriorated. You have to either settle for less effectiveness or sweeten your bid.

Search terms or keywords that embody a lot of intent or interest by searchers can sell for quite high prices per click. *The New York Times* reported that the price of keywords like "life insurance" rose to more than $20 from about $1 between 2002 and 2012.[5] In addition, few positions get a lot of clicks; usually only the top three or four get clicked much. Then, too, SERPs show text ads or text links—just <u>underlined</u> words—which are the least engaging, immersive, or brand-building sorts of ads.

Last, but very important, Internet browsers spend only about 5 percent of their time online at search engines. They spend around 95 percent of their time online at other kinds of sites. So while searchers are much more focused and intent on what they are doing, whether it's research or shopping, their time spent at the search site is very brief.

Buyer Beware

Looking back on the development of search engine marketing, it seems inevitable that innovations such as auction selling, pay-per-click pricing, and metrics like click-through-rate would be widely adopted. These practices seem so aligned with the interests of online advertisers. Indeed, proponents of paid-search advertising have claimed that the advertiser has extraordinary control over its connection to the viewer. The question is: How reliable is that control?

For all the seeming transparency and accountability of paid-search campaigns, advertisers have encountered problems in conducting them. Almost as soon as they began to put ads alongside search engine results, advertisers wondered whether the search results were biased. Rankings have always been done by algorithms, and advertisers have never been comfortable with having a black box determine whether or where their ads would appear. It's a question of whom (or what, in the case of an algorithm) you trust.

In addition, as pay-per-click pricing became established, there was increasing incidence of what became known as *click fraud*. In one version of this scam, a competing company clicks on a paid-search advertiser's link a massive number of times to force the advertiser to pay for the bogus clicks.

Another search-related fraud is page-jacking. That's when content is copied from one site and re-published on another. The web crawlers that are sent out by search engines to detect search terms and log their occurrence are indefatigable indexers. But they are not Sherlock Holmes or copyright attorneys. They can't identify the content that is original or detect an unauthorized copy. Because of the undiscerning nature of the searching and logging conducted by these web crawlers, the search engine company places a link to the plagiarizing site's pages on the SERP. Although the link to the copied content may rank lower on the SERP than the authentic content, it may nevertheless siphon off traffic that would have gone to the site whose content was ripped off.

Another SEM practice where the gray area at times shades into black (sometimes referred to as *black hat SEO*) is called *link buying*. This happens most often in organic search, where advertisers pay to post links near a search term that comes up in editorial content on a web page. Search advertisers—let's say a retailer—have been known to pay bloggers to, for example, publish pages that extol certain categories of merchandise to which the retailer wants to link. This paid-for SEO buzz produces links that ascend in rank as the number of paid-for editorial mentions proliferates. Although search engine companies such as Google and Microsoft deplore the practice, and sometimes actively discourage it (a process known as *Google slapping*), it can be hard to differentiate genuine buzz from counterfeit buzz.

Despite the sizzle of digital search technology, maximizing the effectiveness of search advertising is no slam dunk. The computer can search fast and automatically. But, clearly, a paid search ad campaign can't be run on autopilot.

CHAPTER 3

Auctions and the Development of Paid-Search Advertising

B ack in the late 1990s, paid–search advertising itself was searching for a new business model. It had gone through several stages of business model development. "If search were a religion, it was polytheistic," says Danny Sullivan, founding editor of SearchEngineLand.com.[1]

Initially search engine marketing was a loss leader for portals such as AOL and Yahoo!. In paid search's first generation, search engine companies offered advertisers only the option of buying a paid listing on the SERP, called a *static listing*. Advertisers paid a set fee for the keyword, for the same spot on the SERP, for a set period. Everything was sold in advance, unchangeable, and unresponsive. It was as if the listings had permanent price tags.

SEM's Early Challenges

SEM made a big lurch forward in 1997, when Bill Gross, who founded Idea-lab, a new–business incubator, started GoTo.com, a search engine marketing company. GoTo.com at the outset was a lot like an online yellow pages. However, Gross was bothered by the proliferation of spam online and, especially, in Internet search. Gross recalls that in the late 1990s, as many as half the listings on SERPs might be completely unrelated to your search.[2]

SEM was earning itself a somewhat unsavory reputation. Because it didn't cost an advertiser anything to be reported on SERPs with an organic listing (a listing whose link led to the search term on an editorial page), sleazy, bait-and-switch websites proliferated. Users who clicked on links on those sites and submitted their contact information at times would be sent invoices. Many unwittingly paid the bills, even though they had received no goods or services.

During the same period, display advertising on the Internet often was inhospitable, especially to smaller advertisers. Selling online ads resembled selling print ads, which were sold predominantly by direct sales forces. Often they imposed hard-to-meet minimum order sizes and charged high fixed prices denominated in cost-per-thousand impressions (CPMs).

"It was a big players' game," says Tim Cadogan, CEO of OpenX Technologies, an operator of an online exchange, and, from 1999 to 2003, a senior executive at GoTo.com. "Smaller companies had no way to advertise economically on the web. They had no effective voice."

The spamming, especially, irritated Gross. "There was a dramatic decline in the quality of search results," he explained. His first try at fixing the problem, which occupied him for four or five months in 1997, was to set up a paid-search venture in which human curator-editors would evaluate and approve the legitimate sites before they were posted on the SERP. This attempt failed dismally. There was no way that Gross's human watchdogs could keep up with the traffic and the proliferation of sleazy spammers.

"There were all these kludgy tricks [spammers] were playing to game the system," says Gross. "By November 1997 we realized that our solution was beautiful, but not scalable."

Gross lamented this decline in search quality. One day late in December 1997, Gross was sitting in his office at Idealab with several of his staff-ers. All of them were grousing about how frustrated they were that their effort to reform paid search had failed. Gross listened absentmindedly to their kvetching. He, too, was frustrated and a bit humiliated by the failure of the venture. Then he noticed a set of yellow pages lying around his of-fice. It was a search technology, too, he realized, but just an old-fashioned, analog one. He had a thought: You never get spam in the yellow pages. Why? Suddenly it occurred to him that it was because advertisers *paid* for their display ads in the yellow pages. No one got a display ad for nothing.

All advertisers knew that everyone paid for their yellow pages display ads and that how much they paid determined how big the ad was. It was all completely transparent. There was what publishers call a *rate card*, a document with retail prices stipulated. A full-page ad costs so much. A sixteenth-page ad costs around one-sixteenth as much. You get what you pay for. Why not apply that principle to paid search? Gross wondered. Next, he took his idea a step further. Instead of a rate card, why not cre-ate an *auction?* he asked himself. Being forced to pay would exclude the spammers, and you could use the bids as a way to sort advertisers on the SERP. The highest bidder would appear at the top of the column—the most conspicuous and desirable location—on the SERP. Gross still recalls the excitement he felt when he told his staff the idea. The buzz didn't last very long. His crew shot the idea down and told him to forget it.

But Gross had a number of start-ups operating in Idealab's building. All of them were tiny companies, and all of them advertised online. Gross walked around the building and asked them what they, as advertisers, thought of the idea. They all loved it.

"All of our companies were doing banner ads on the web," Gross says. "So I asked them, 'What are you paying for a person to come to your site?'"

Many did not know. "But, when we said, 'How would you like to pay exactly what it's worth to you for them to come to your site?,' they were thrilled." That vision was the start of a frenzy of development at Idealab.

Gross wanted to present the auction idea at the TED (Technology, Entertainment, and Design) conference in Monterey, California, on February 28, 1998.

While the new way of doing business was being developed, Gross had his salespeople go out and sign up charter advertisers, who would demonstrate the feasibility and economic advantages of the approach. Pretty quickly, they got about one hundred advertisers. All were tiny companies. Gross then had a few salespeople focus on getting at least ten big advertisers to sign up. Eventually, they got notable firms such as Amazon, Toyota, and About.com to sign up, and Gross's salespeople flaunted the big names when they told other potential advertisers about the new venture.

Then, unexpectedly, just a few days before the TED conference, several of the big marquee advertisers pulled out. Toyota, Amazon, and others were worried that GoTo's SERPs would display what they bid. This was too much transparency for them. They canceled, and Gross worried that their defections would have a snowball effect on other advertisers.

When he took the stage at TED a few days later to describe his terrific new brainchild, Gross had forebodings that the concept was falling apart even before it was officially announced. He saw a number of influential people in the audience, among them Jeff Bezos, CEO of Amazon, and Scott Kurnit, CEO of About.com. Panning the room after he finished his talk, he thought he saw the sort of body language that indicated disapproval. No high fives, no fist pumps. He remembers feeling pretty demoralized.

After some polite-but-strained chitchat outside the auditorium, Gross trudged back to the hotel. By chance, he got into the same elevator as Bezos was in.

"Terrific presentation," Gross recalls Bezos saying to him.

Gross couldn't believe what he was hearing. "What are you talking about?" he asked Bezos. "You pulled the plug on us three days ago."

Now it was Bezos's turn to be incredulous. As it happened, the decision to pull out of the new paid-search auction-pricing regimen had been made by someone lower down in the Amazon hierarchy. Bezos had no clue. He assured Gross that he would get Amazon back working with him.

That moment was the beginning of true pay-for-performance ad sales in paid-search advertising.

Paid-Search Auctions

They worked like this. An advertiser chose as its search term a specific keyword or phrase and placed a bid on that term. The advertiser submitted an ad for the term. GoTo's editors checked it for relevance. If the ad was accepted, it was shown when a user searched for the term.[3] However, the auction did *not* eliminate other bidders. This was not a winner-take-all competition. Paid-search advertising became accessible to all advertisers, big and small. Lower bidders' ads were also presented on the SERP, but in descending prominence. The lower the bid, the lower that advertiser's ad ranked. According to Andrew Ellam and Marco Ottaviani, "When the user clicked on an ad, the advertiser was billed the amount of their bid. A user might click on more than one ad—in which case more than one advertiser would be billed—or on none."[4]

"This was a 'rupture point,'" says Cadogan from OpenX. "Nothing like that existed before. It was a brand new business model. GoTo invented paid search."

The new model encouraged marketers, especially those at smaller firms. It didn't burden them with too much risk. The cost of entry was low. Advertisers could bid a penny. That wouldn't get their link featured prominently, near the top of the stack, but no matter how meager their budget, they could be in the game on a SERP.

GoTo's new ad sales regimen was targeted, self-service (that is, there was no intermediation by a direct sales force), advertisers named their price, and the deal could be changed at any time, which meant bidders could raise or lower their bids as the market or their circumstances changed.

At times, this auction selling could be advantageously *elastic*. When bids and rankings were bunched close together and competitors were not changing bids in response, sometimes a very small increase in a bid could greatly improve an ad's rank and lead to big improvements in traffic and clicks.

GoTo's innovation made paid-search advertising simple and transparent. Advertisers knew what they were bidding, and they could see how much they would rise in rank by how much they raised their bid. They could compare what they were doing with what others were doing; in that way, they could make an educated guess about what others were bidding and develop a bidding strategy. "[Advertisers could] constantly monitor or modify their performance, daily if they wished," says Cadogan. Accessible and fair as this new auction-selling model may have been, GoTo's business could not cruise along as if it were a bike being ridden with no hands on the bars. GoTo may have been a scrappy little start-up with new ideas, but, to succeed, it had to grow itself from a minnow to the biggest fish in the pond before a bigger fish could swallow it. It had invented the new model. Commercializing it was another thing entirely. As with other Internet businesses, even those blessed with brilliantly innovative technologies or breakthrough business models, the problem was achieving scale.

Fortunately, 1998 saw the arrival at GoTo of Ted Meisel, who became one of the pioneers of paid search. A Stanford-educated lawyer, Meisel had worked as a McKinsey strategy consultant before he came to GoTo as chief operating officer. Meisel realized that crucial to GoTo's success was getting much more traffic from Internet searchers. Even though its focus was on search, GoTo wasn't getting anywhere near the growth in traffic it needed.

Getting that scale, and in a hurry, was a complicated challenge for Meisel to manage. GoTo had to pull off three difficult initiatives at the same time: (1) getting search adopted by advertisers, (2) getting much more search business, and (3) making sure that GoTo and its partners (the portals from which it got the searches) fulfilled their commitments to advertisers (which included billing them correctly).

Search advertising was new to advertisers. It required an awful lot of explanation. Search wasn't an important part of most advertisers' campaigns then. From 1997 to 1998, display advertising, sold on a CPM basis, and other forms of sponsorship accounted for 80 to 90 percent of ad sales on the Internet.

"The promise of [advertising on] the Internet," says Meisel, who now is a senior adviser at the private equity firm Elevation Partners, "was to [enable] the right ad to be delivered to the right person at the right time for the right price."

To fulfill that promise to advertisers and get search adopted, Meisel's sales pitch spotlighted the fairness of the auction model. "We were the first to say that the right price was decided by the advertiser," says Meisel, and the right price was "what was bid."

Ensuring that the ad was delivered to the right person was the easy part. In search advertising, the right person is defined by what the person is looking for.

Getting search traffic was the big hurdle. GoTo wasn't getting enough. So Meisel went to the big portals (for example, AOL and Yahoo!) and offered to take over their search engine function. In return, he offered to share a portion of the search ad revenues.

This was a tough sell. Not surprisingly, the big portals thought of the customers as theirs. Why share them with GoTo? Why not get 100 percent of the search ad revenues from those users? These questions were understandable, if a bit self-deluding. Both the portals and Meisel knew that the portals weren't making much money from search. In their hands, it had been a loss leader.

On the other hand, GoTo was a pipsqueak. Why expect it to do any better? Actually, there were several reasons. In the first place, it was a pipsqueak with a dramatically different and appealing ad sales model. Second, it was a pipsqueak that was focusing 24/7 on search. Third—and very attention-getting—it was a pipsqueak offering not only to share search ad revenues but also to give the portals annual ad revenue *guarantees*.

From one perspective, these offers appeared disconcertingly grandiose, like someone using food stamps to go into a catering business. In 1998, when GoTo grossed less than a million dollars, Meisel was offering multi-year deals with revenue guarantees of from $20 million to $30 million to portals such as MSN, Yahoo!, and EarthLink. It offered an annual guarantee of $50 million to AOL.

According to those who were party to the negotiations, Meisel was always calm, cool, very precise, and patient. He certainly acted like someone who knew what he was talking about, yet he was offering multiyear revenue guarantees that, in the aggregate, were in the hundreds of millions of dollars. Not only was Meisel betting all the chips GoTo had, he was betting chips he thought he'd be getting from some undiscovered galaxy.

For someone who took a skeptical, "show-me-the-money" squint at them, these deals were like the *Titanic* manufacturing its own iceberg. Who knew whether the Internet would keep growing? Unbeknownst to any of the negotiators, the dot-com bust and September 11 terrorist attacks were just around the corner.

"What we were doing was a little bit heretical," says Meisel. "We didn't have a proprietary algorithm. Our share of the consumer search [business] was only 5 percent."

But Meisel was betting the company in another sense that was both strategic and compelling. It was only by and because of such "syndication" deals that GoTo would be able to grow, and grow quickly.

"Many were skeptical that advertising could be sold that way," admits Meisel. "But the key innovation of our model was that we initiated competition for prominence on the SERP. We bridged the gap between the way publishers wanted to price and the way advertisers wanted to price. We made it easy for advertisers to buy. And we'd say, 'Try it for a month to see if it works for you.'"

The portals signed up, and then the advertisers did. Thereafter, whenever anyone began a search at the portal, the search request was instantaneously sent over to GoTo, which conducted the search and then published the results on the SERP at the portal. Most users thought that they were getting a Yahoo! search or an AOL search.

With syndication deals in hand, Meisel, Cadogan, and others to whom Gross had turned over the management of GoTo then had to struggle to manage growth that felt like a five–year–long rocket launch. From less than $1 million in revenues in 1998, GoTo rocketed to around $20 million in 1999. Revenues quadrupled in 2000, to around $80 million. Then they more than tripled, to $250 million in 2001, and more than doubled in 2002, to $650 million. In the first five years that Meisel ran GoTo, which changed its name to Overture Services, Inc., in 2001, the company grew to more than $1 billion in sales (2003).

Fulfillment, in ad serving and billing, was a constant challenge. Overture asked advertisers, in effect, to give them their credit cards. "We ran it like an ATM," says Meisel. "They gave us an amount of money and we debited their account." As growth became exponential, Overture was running an order of magnitude more transactions than a credit card network. Every time an Internet user clicked on a link or ad on a SERP, it was an ad sales transaction. Overture's bookkeeping was like keeping track not only of all the butterflies in the world but also of how many times they beat their wings. "We had to do it minute by minute," says Meisel. "Credit card issuers only have to reconcile at the end of the month."

Pay–per–click ad sales were becoming a reality on the Internet. Search engine marketing surpassed (made more money annually) than the business of selling display advertising beginning in 2003, to become the dominant form of online advertising. (By comparison, during this time, click–through rates for display advertising had fallen from above 5 percent to less than half a percent by 2001.[5]) This may have been the first true pay–for–performance advertising. "The profits that were being generated by search companies like [Overture] helped wake people up to the fact that something huge was going on," says Danny Sullivan.[6]

While Meisel held the reins, Overture became the biggest paid–search firm in the world, as well as the most innovative. It introduced the Internet to the utility of auction selling and pay-per-click pricing, and it also created a business model that made the company not only feasible but also immensely profitable. In five years, Overture had become the superpower of paid-search advertising. In July 2003, Yahoo! announced that it would acquire Overture for $1.63 billion.

So where was Google?

CHAPTER 4

The Google Eclipse

Nowadays Google is so widely acknowledged as the Goliath of the Internet, it's hard to recall that while Overture was morphing Incredible Hulk–like, Google was the wimpy kid. But it was a wimpy kid with some assets that gave it advantages even against a competitor as big and well funded as Overture.

Overture didn't have a proprietary search algorithm. Google had a proprietary algorithm that drove traffic to Google. Its search algorithm became celebrated. By contrast, Overture was, in effect, renting traffic from the portals. Overture was giving portals up to 70 percent or more of the revenues it received. Google didn't have to pay for the traffic as Overture did.

Google also had an edge when it came to branding. Many users may have found searching at the portals satisfactory, but Overture, which handled the search traffic, usually didn't get credit for it. It was functioning in the background most of the time. It was toiling in well-paid obscurity doing what were generic searches. Meanwhile, Google was becoming a search brand. Its name became synonymous with searching. *Google* became a verb.

Google had its own traffic and its own brand. Google was not only gaining huge increases in traffic, it was keeping 100 percent of the revenues it got from advertising. Google didn't have to share revenues with portals—a big and continuing advantage over Overture. Having to rent traffic eroded Overture's profitability. Meanwhile, the competition from Google became tougher. Even when it was smaller than Overture, Google could keep more of the money it made per search, which helped cut Overture's size advantage as Google was fighting an uphill battle.

The AdWords Advantage

In February 2002, while Overture's market share was still bigger than Google's, Google introduced a new pricing regimen called AdWords Select. The new approach retained auction bidding on search terms but with some key differences. Whereas Overture had ranked search advertisers simply according to how high their bids were and charged them the amount they had bid per click, Google ranked advertisers based on their bid price multiplied by the click-through rate of their links. The advertiser's SERP ranking was adjusted as its ad's CTR changed. This meant that an advertiser that bid less than the highest price might get the top rank.

It worked like this. Suppose Google had two advertisers, A and B. A bids $5 for a given search term for a given period. B bids $10 for the same search term for the same period. Now suppose that A has a click-through rate of 0.4 and B has a CTR of 0.1, which Google knows based on its previous experience with the bidders. Google would get $2 from A ($5 × 0.4) vs. $1 from B ($10 × 0.1). Because it would get more money from featuring A's ad (or link) more prominently than B's ad (or link) for that search term, Google would give A top rank even though it bid less per click for the term. Overture would have given top rank to B.

The AdWords Select pricing policy became a competitive advantage, although it was more complicated and variable than Overture's simpler ranking by bid price and also less transparent. Google didn't tell advertisers what everyone else was bidding. Nevertheless, the policy was seen to be more fair and productive. Customers might pay more in total at times, even though they may have bid less per click than another bidder, but they would be paying the higher rate for advertising that was working better. They were paying more for advertising that was more productive because its click–through rate was higher.

The way Google set things up, the advantage continued to improve for bigger–spending advertisers with better ads. The more prominent their rank, the higher the click–through rate was. The higher the click–through rate, the more productive the ad was. Google still owned the casino, but the high rollers felt they had a bigger and continuing edge against other advertisers.

Google's auction was also conducted differently from Overture's. It was (and still is) what is called a *second-price auction*, which means that bidders did not pay the actual amount of their bid. Instead, they paid one penny more than the bid immediately below theirs. Suppose that five advertisers bid 50¢, 33¢, 28¢, 17¢, and 12¢ to be listed alongside a search term for a specific period of time. They would actually be charged 34¢, 29¢, 18¢, 13¢, and 12¢. This looks as if it would reduce the total amount that Google could realize from such an auction, but, in 1961, William Vickrey, a Nobel Prize–winning economist at Columbia University, proved mathematically that second–price auctions make sellers just as much money as the more familiar auctions used to sell art masterpieces (which are winner–take–all and known as *English auctions*). Second–price auctions for rankings on the Google SERP were not winner–take–all. Almost all bidders[1] were ranked and paid for every click they got. Second–price auctions also provided buyers with the simplest optimal bidding strategy. (For more on types of auctions and optimal bidding strategies, see Chapter 7 on real-time bidding for display ad impressions.)

As advertisers became familiar with Google's new system, they saw it as advantageous to both Google and themselves. AdWords pricing enabled them to get a higher rank while bidding less, even though they paid more in total. Let's say that someone bought the search term "car insurance" on Google. The buyer might have paid as much as $25 a click, a really pricey keyword. But such a term could achieve a click-through rate of as high as 50 percent. For every one thousand viewers who saw the results for the term, five hundred clicked on it. That might produce an effective CPM (eCPM) of $12,500 for Google (500 clickers × $25 per click = $12,500). By comparison, a really high-priced ad on a premium website might sell for a $100 eCPM.

Paying more in total seemed fair because it resulted in advertising that was more productive (because the ads were ranked higher and got higher click-through rates). Advertisers didn't mind that Google's system was a better way (for Google) of monetizing the search results on the SERP, if their ad dollars were working harder for them, too. As a result, more advertisers gravitated to Google.

Moreover, during this period portals such as Yahoo! loaded their landing pages with lots of advertising. Google, which kept 100 percent of the revenues from the searches it conducted and got more revenue per search because of the AdWords pricing system, ran a less cluttered page.

By the end of 2002, Google's market share had surpassed that of Overture. It became, and remains, the dominant player in paid-search advertising.

How dominant? So dominant it would be a misleading understatement to call Google "the OPEC of paid-search advertising." On its best oil-crisis-fomenting day, OPEC is a little schoolyard bully compared to Google. In 2013, according to estimates by eMarketer, Google's $14.1 billion search ad revenues amounted to *over 70 percent* of the year's $19.9 billion total U.S. spending for search.[2] OPEC members—collectively—are responsible for only about 40 percent of world oil production.[3]

Paid Search and the Future of Google

But there is one sense in which Google is very much like the oil cartel. It is focused overwhelmingly on one market. Even with its various diversifications (browser, web applications, Android mobile phones), approximately 91 percent of Google's 2013 revenues came from advertising[4] and 82.4 percent of those ad revenues came from paid search.[5] According to SearchEngineLand.com, in December 2013, Google conducted 67.3 percent of all searches done in the United States.[6]

In addition to being the alpha dog, the porch Google sits on is, for the time being, the sweet spot in online advertising. Search advertising is forecast to continue to outsell display until 2015.[7]

So far, Google hasn't been able to diversify itself substantially enough for the diversification to be material. That isn't a problem now. Usually, dominance is an advantage. But it could mean that Google will be affected more emphatically than other search companies by changes that may constrain the search market. Direct-response advertisers in the United States, many of which build their entire marketing campaigns around search and are its heaviest users, may come to believe that we are approaching a limit on how much of the paid-search advertising extant is really effective. Let's look, for comparison, at the yellow pages business. In a big city like New York, the yellow pages contain numerous pages of listings with associated display ads for lawyers. The yellow pages also contain page after page of listings and ads devoted solely to divorce lawyers. Not all those ads for divorce lawyers are productive, but lots of lawyers buy them because they believe that, if they didn't, they would be at a competitive disadvantage. Whether warranted or not, such concerns about vulnerability help keep the yellow pages display ad business ticking along.

Such concerns don't carry over to paid search. Search engine companies can't book comparably long lists of links because bidders know very well that only the most prominent links (those at the top of the stack) are going to be clicked on. That drives up the price for the top links, but it also discourages bidding for links below the top tier. That could impose a limit on the growth of productive links for paid search.

Of course, there are other countervailing factors driving the expansion of paid-search advertising. One factor is the overall ascendancy of digital advertising in general. Since 2010, online ad spending surpassed newspaper advertising spending. That made Internet advertising second only to TV among measured media.[8] A Bain.com article reports, "Much of the projected growth will come from direct-response advertising—in particular, search. This suits advertisers seeking an immediate, measurable return on investment (ROI), usually in the form of web site traffic and sales transactions."[9]

According to a study by Borrell Associates, the adversity of the most recent recession has accelerated the migration to online advertising, especially for small and medium-size businesses (SMBs). "The harsh economic environment has caused them to re-evaluate longstanding practices of relying on yellow pages, newspapers, radio, and direct mail to reach consumers. Over the next five years, their ad spending on these four legacy media alone [is] forecast to fall 19 percent, representing average annual declines of $3.4 billion. Meanwhile, spending on paid search by local advertisers is forecast to rise 39 percent, representing average annual increases of $242 million."[10] All these trends have, in fact, been realized, and marketers have spent more money on direct-response-like digital search ads every year from 2003 to 2013.[11]

Paid-search advertising has been the largest part of that.

How well search engine marketing performs is not certain, even if it grows enormously and Google grows with it. Search engine marketing has to be both creative and well managed, just like display advertising. If the experience of brand advertisers with ad networks (see Chapter 5) is any indication of what to expect from the future of search advertising, there is going to be a long learning curve before brand marketers learn how to move the needle with SEM.

CHAPTER 5

Display Advertising and the Advent of Ad Networks

The saga of free enterprise tells us that markets strive for efficiency. Buyers and sellers tolerate intermediaries as a "necessary" evil. Intermediaries, we are told, skim money that could have gone to the seller or saved the buyer some cash. Instead, they raise prices and take profits when they resell stuff they didn't create. Without these pesky, cagey intermediaries buying low and selling high, prices would tend toward some value that is described as "natural," "true," or in some sense appropriate. It's the inexorable destiny of such intermediaries to be ousted from their positions. Economists call being eliminated this way *disintermediation*.

That's the story, anyway. Here on Planet Earth, it's more complicated.[1] The way things work is not so tidy, efficient, and ideal. That has certainly been true of the market for digital display media.

In the development of online advertising, the ad networks were the in-termediaries, taking profits and raising prices downstream. Many in digital advertising—especially those who run online ad exchanges—believe things would be better if there were no ad networks clogging up what could be an automated media allocation process.

Whether ad networks have been a necessary evil or merely an earlier stage in the development of the market for digital display advertising that inevitably will disappear, online advertising probably could not have arisen without them. Technology may provide leaps of imaginative innovation—that certainly has been true for digital media—but new industries need their training wheels.

In Chapter 1, I described the online advertising ecosystem as being crowded with intermediaries. To keep things clear, I presented a deliberately simplified taxonomy of the intermediaries and likened the ecosystem to a toll road. As I described, in the early days of online advertising publishers weren't very familiar with or adept at selling their impressions and advertisers often lacked the technological expertise to handle the buying in a well-informed, selective, and advantageous way.

While this ecosystem was no doubt inefficient, especially because it raised prices downstream, it would be a big mistake to look at all those intermediaries as unnecessary. This was a formative period in the development of the online advertising business, and there was a lot to be learned all around.

The Internet is a gigantic engine for generating content, providing services, and creating business opportunity worldwide. But handling all that the new medium offers has not been easy. The stupendous scale in terms of usage and the breathtaking speed of the technology are a completely new and potent combination in advertising.

All that daunting newness has been exacerbated because it has rested much of the time on an economically unstable foundation. That instability has been an ever-present and ever-threatening risk. Why unstable? Because of the exponential proliferation of websites and the web pages they publish,[2] this industry has been characterized by an oversupply of online media. Supply has exceeded demand for much of the industry's history. Consider: A zillion web page views presented in a year times, let's say, two ads per page. On average each of us is exposed (online and offline) to hundreds of ads per day.

The supply of ads online is always available, but it's hyperfragmented. Zillions of web pages and moments when users are viewing a particular page amount to a complicated buying exercise for advertisers. "Media fragmentation, driven by a dramatic uptick in web sites in the last decade, made it increasingly difficult for buyers to manage the multitude of individual publisher buys necessary to meet marketers' needs," say Forrester analysts Joanna O'Connell and Michael Greene.[3]

Moreover, online media is perishable. Online publishers, whatever their pretensions about quality and expectations of getting premium prices, feel a strong imperative to sell what they have. The ad can be displayed to users only when they are viewing a web page, and they may click away in the next moment. Better to get something rather than nothing—right?—if you can capture users' split second of engagement and attention. And you have to get that money when you can.

With that vision in publishers' minds of how perishable an impression is, having a buyer—even if it is an intermediary—upon which publishers could depend to take their fleeting ad impressions seemed far better than distributing web pages with white spaces where the paid ads might be. Hence, the ad networks. Hence, the "necessary" evil.

When supply far exceeds demand, what might at first appear to be an orderly, if inefficient, market can in a moment degenerate into a missed opportunity of unsold or misallocated impressions and disappointed expectations.

Granted, that's not as calamitous as a meltdown at a nuclear power plant. But it's a lot of hurt to have to face when you come in to work each day.

At the beginning of Internet advertising, it was extremely labor-intensive for ad agencies to buy online impressions. Agencies had to deliver for their advertiser-clients in two ways. First, they had to find the right users to whom to show their ads. Second, they had to find enough of them to create something like a mass audience. Marketers, long used to buying big TV or radio audiences or the readerships of large-circulation newspapers or magazines, weren't used to buying their audiences in little bits and pieces from a multitude of suppliers (all those separate websites). So ad agencies also had to deliver *scale*: big numbers of digital users. Without scale, advertisers feared their voices wouldn't be heard in a universe as fragmented and chaotically cluttered as the Internet.

However, the possibility that you could create a mass audience by buying impressions directly from the websites—let's call that "do-it-yourself aggregation"—seemed pretty dubious. Approaching all those sites directly and individually would have amounted to a gigantic Easter egg hunt for the ad agencies.

That's not the way they were used to buying media. Before the advent of online media buying, giant advertising holding companies would aggregate the media buying for all their ad agencies, make mass buys, and drive down prices because they had so much clout and publishers wanted so badly to make deals with them. Deals were struck through negotiation. Personal relationships were crucial to getting deals negotiated and approved by decision makers on both sides of the transaction. Ad buying, placement, and the assessment of the effectiveness of those ad placements were handled by people—teams of people. Those teams of media buyers had no experience buying from a multitude of website publishers, and they were skeptical that it would be useful (at least for the advancement of their careers) to become familiar with juggling all those suppliers[4] with their audience slivers. Compared to their radio, TV, or mass-market print advertising, online advertising was, at the outset, less significant than the tail of their advertising dog.

Things were just as frustrating and unfeasible on the sell side. Few publishing companies had—or were willing to go to the effort and expense of developing—sales forces to sell their digital media. In the early days, publishers viewed their Internet media as a low-value add-on to their print media businesses. They were selling the tiny tail of their media dog.

Because of the widespread lack of experience in managing the power of all that scale and speed as well as the early stages of learning how to use it effectively, there was compelling value in finding someone to help you handle it. The ad networks got a foothold because they offered a much more efficient way to buy digital media.

By using ad networks, ad agencies could buy lots of impressions and get a large audience without having to conduct a scavenger hunt for each campaign. One-stop shopping. They could send the ad network one insertion order (a contract for the media buy that, in effect, requisitions a particular audience) and later pay one bill.

Training Wheels

Also important, ad agency media buyers and their advertiser–clients got to experience the at times illusory comfort that they were managing a process that was the advertising equivalent of trying to manage a herd of cattle. So, for the same reason that ranchers build corrals and conduct cattle drives, ad networks thrived. They collected all that live, perishable merchandise that was threatening to stray or stay behind and sent it where it needed to go. It's not surprising that ad networks were viewed as indispensable. They took huge amounts of pain out of media buying. They made it more trouble-free and efficient.

DoubleClick personified that industry–inventing opportunity. When Wenda Harris Millard, who had been a top magazine publishing executive, joined the new company in 1996, it had 12 people and sales of around $50,000 (by Millard's guesstimate). After four years, DoubleClick had 3,200 people in twenty-three countries producing $500 million in revenues, around 80 percent of that from sales of media for advertising.

Ad networks achieved this enormous growth by taking a bunch of impressions that publishers thought they were not going to be able to unload (remnant inventory) and turning them, seemingly magically, into substantial, if not mass, audiences.

There have been numerous kinds of ad networks. Some resold media from only one type of publication—for example, just travel or auto enthusiast sites. Others resold media from publications on a variety of subjects but only from premium publishers. A third type emphasized impressions reaching only a given audience—say, affluent users—wherever they might be found. Still other networks offered a mix of impressions at dirt-cheap prices, but you couldn't be selective about where your ad appeared. You just had to let the ad network reach into its grab bag for you, accept its media placements, and hope something paid off. Those ad networks were the digital equivalent of dollar stores. All but the last of these ad network types claimed somehow (see following discussion) to optimize their ad placements.

But if ad networks helped make media buying more trouble free and efficient for advertisers—and took a big amount of the risk off the publishers' shoulders—the services and solutions they offered came with their own set of problems.

Bumps in the Road

Almost from the beginning, problems with ad networks emerged. The audiences put together by ad networks were sizable, but that didn't assure advertisers that the members of these audiences were the right viewers for their ads, especially when the purpose of the ad was to build the brand. Where brand building and developing brand loyalty are concerned, size isn't everything. Certainly, scale is necessary. But scale is not enough.

A big problem was inappropriate placements. Once networks bought big amounts of digital publishers' remnant impressions, even if they bought them for breathtakingly low prices, they were under the same imperative that publishers were. They needed to sell these impressions, and ad networks could be much less choosy than advertisers were about where they placed the ads.

Although ad networks occasionally provided advertisers with a list of the sites on which the ads would appear, marketers had no way of knowing where and when their ads would appear and to whom they were presented.

So, for example, a display ad for a cruise ship company might appear on a web page containing a story about an outbreak of dysentery among the passengers of a cruise ship or on a web page with a story about the sinking of a cruise ship. Misplacements like these were a cruise line operator's nightmare. If the advertiser's purpose was to promote a brand, these missteps posed the continual threat of cheapening the brand. Granted, such problems occur in other ad media, but there is a big difference when it occurs in a new medium that is trying to establish its bona fides.

Once the ad network made the deal to buy the impressions from the publisher, neither the advertiser nor the publisher had ultimate control over where the ads appeared. It was a big exercise in "trust me," with the ad network in control. The ad networks had to sell as many of the impressions they had in inventory as they could, which meant that the needs of the advertiser might be of lower priority than their own, often with counterproductive and at times disastrous results. Such instances did not represent what anyone meant by the term *optimization*.

Optimization was conjectural or inferential at best. The lack of information about placement also hampered advertisers and their agencies from assessing the effectiveness of their campaigns. Marketers might be able to determine how well their campaigns were working overall, but they had no way of knowing which ad impressions were having the impact they wanted and which were not working well. This prevented them from fine-tuning their advertising so as to make the most of it.

Another problem was the secrecy that prevailed about pricing. There was a lot of backroom deal making before the ad network deployed its media on behalf of an advertiser or its agency.[5] The advertiser or its ad agency didn't know what the ad network paid for the media impressions it was reselling and, therefore, had no way of determining the real value of the media. This was an exercise in taking black-box optimization and exacerbating it with black-box pricing. Of course, such problems crop up in any ad medium, but these were stumbling blocks that plagued a new medium trying to become adopted.

The only thing that advertisers and their agencies knew for certain was that the ad network had bought the media from the publisher for less than the ad agency paid the ad network for it. They knew that the ad network was making a profit selling it to them. This created the nagging conjecture that they could have bought the same media directly from the web publisher for less than they paid the ad network. The profit the ad network made, whatever it was, was a sticking point throughout the market, and it bred a certain rancor. Both the advertisers and the publishers begrudged it.

This situation with intermediaries also led to "channel conflict." That is, it led advertisers to be disgruntled about the higher prices they paid when they did buy impressions *directly* from so-called premium publishers. Because they knew that intermediaries were making profits with the prices they were charging, advertisers, who realized that they could buy remnant impressions for much lower prices from ad networks, wondered why they should pay premium prices buying directly from publishers. Why pay premium prices when I can get your remnant from an ad network much cheaper? the advertisers thought.

That raised doubts in advertisers' minds about the entire pricing structure. If intermediaries were profitable, then the publishers must be charging far too much for the space they sold directly to them, the advertisers thought. The profits that ad networks made were evidence that publishers were selling impressions to ad networks for much lower prices than they were charging advertisers who bought directly from the publishers. That was just an inference, of course, but, as with jealousy, it did not have to be confirmed rigorously to poison the relationship.

This was a business relationship that was fraught with invidious conjectures at the outset. Advertisers are still depending on someone else—in this case, the ad network—to gather the audience and assure them that a particular group of viewers of their ad is going to be most advantageous.

Why believe them? As with publishers, the ad networks were up against an imperative to sell not only the impressions that are optimal for the advertiser but all the impressions they had bought. Wouldn't it have been better for the advertiser to select the audience itself and be completely assured about the audience for their advertising? Furthermore, wouldn't it have been better for the advertiser to determine the sensible value of and influence the price paid for the media?

There had to be some alternative to this market in which intermediaries were proliferating and profiting.

That brings us to real-time bidding.

CHAPTER 6

Real-Time Bidding and the Transformation of Online Advertising

Buying online media for display advertising using real–time bidding is a big deal. RTB is one of the hottest new technologies that marketers and their ad agencies ever got their hands on. It'll take a bit of explaining.

A number of companies such as Google and OpenX have created on-line exchanges that sell online media placement where advertisers can present their display ads.

Since 2010, digital advertising has witnessed the advent of real–time auctions on online exchanges.

Chapter 3 described how GoTo.com developed online auctions to sell paid–search advertising—ads that appeared when a person used a search engine such as Yahoo!, AOL, or Google. Those auctions were a major advance in the technology of online advertising. But those auctions occurred *before* the search queries were made by the user. The bidding for those placements might have been conducted months earlier. By contrast, real–time bidding for display ads is so fast that all the automated auctions and placements happen in the event in two-tenths of a second—after the user has requested the web page but before the page is delivered to the user. (See Chapter 7 for a step-by-step description of how this happens.)

But real-time bidding for display ads is important for more than its blistering speed. Real-time auctions are an improvement in the fundamentals of selling online display advertising for a number of reasons: (1) They lay the foundation for a transformation in online advertising, (2) they have cranked up the growth of display advertising, and (3) in less than four years, they have begun to have effects that will become more noteworthy as advertising on mobile devices becomes widespread.

RTB Changes the Relationship Among Advertisers, Sellers, and Customers

Real-time auctions transform the relationship among advertisers, publishers, and prospective customers. To get a sense of how dramatic a change this is, contrast it with advertising on a billboard beside a busy highway. What does the advertiser know about those viewers? Just that they are drivers or bus riders. With regard to audience selection, using that highway billboard is a crapshoot.

Although audience aggregation in online advertising is better than that billboard, in many instances it hasn't been much better informed. In the past, online advertisers had to depend upon publishers to get their audience members together. They had to trust that the audience segments offered by publishers would prove to be advantageous. With real-time bidding they don't have to take that on faith.

By using real-time bidding systems, advertisers are buying the right to present their ads to *each individual user*. Advertisers no longer have to buy their audiences like bunches of grapes. No more bulk buys.

Despite their speed, online auctions give advertisers the chance to decide whether a given user is the right sort of person to whom to present a given ad. Advertisers can select who suits them by the dynamic act of deciding *which* users to bid for. Advertisers have the chance to create their optimal audience. They make their own decisions rather than relying on an intermediary to make decisions for them.

Furthermore, advertisers can be as selective as they wish about their ad spending because they decide how much to bid. That means a more deliberate selection of users to whom the ad appears—maybe even a more well-informed one; certainly a more transparent one.

As a result, real-time bidding radically changes the old, passive audience aggregation paradigm. In a way, it's similar to the purchase of individual songs—a single track rather than the whole CD—by means of a music service such as iTunes. The advertiser buys only what it wants, by the piece. The audience is analogous to the advertiser's playlist.

Many advertisers know a lot about their customers. They are sitting on mountains of data about their customers in their own databases (called *first-party data*). With real-time bidding systems, they can now use that data—what is, in effect, the viewing or shopping preferences and behavior of their customers—to determine their optimal audience. Advertisers can select exactly the people to whom they wish their ads to appear. They can construct their audience and they can make it as large as they think it needs to be.

"Buying individual impressions—that is a massive shift," says Philip Smolin, the senior vice president for strategy at Turn, Inc., a marketing software and analytics platform for brands and agencies. "After a hundred years of using content [that is, the content of the publication in which the ad has appeared or will appear] as a proxy for audience, marketers could now target audiences directly."

An advertiser may choose to work with a publisher, ad network, or demand-side platform to put its audience together. But it no longer has to passively and uncritically rely on them to prefabricate an audience and deliver it in a black box. With the advent of real-time bidding on online exchanges, the advertiser can be actively involved in the audience-aggregation process and can ascertain for itself that the audience it is buying consists of potential customers it believes are the most advantageous because it can select them for itself, if it wishes.

RTB's Impact on the Cost of Advertising

Ads bought by real-time bidding also can be cheaper. Advertisers no longer have to buy impressions at prices preset by publishers. Auction bidding can drive prices down when the supply of impressions greatly exceeds the demand, which has often been true in Internet publishing. In addition, the automated auctions cut out intermediaries such as ad networks and eliminate their markup.

This sort of selling can also cut costs for publishers. Tedious, time-consuming functions that had been handled by salespeople and support staff today can be replaced by automated auctions, so that salespeople can operate more effectively and on a consultative basis with their best customers. In many cases, a few customers provide most of a publisher's revenues. There is much to be gained from having senior salespeople pay lots of attention to key accounts while numerous small accounts buy their impressions in an automated way using real-time bidding. That improves the efficacy of the sales function while it cuts unnecessary overhead. Such efficiencies drive down the cost of media for advertisers while making more impressions more profitable for the publisher.

In addition to sometimes cutting prices, real-time auctions also enable advertisers to more precisely determine the value of audience members. Previously, audience members were sold in groups. Publishers, not advertisers, decided how to split up their audiences into different parts. Audience segments were sold en masse at prenegotiated prices. Of course, the diverse users in the audiences, even those within a given audience segment, were not all equally valuable for any given marketing initiative. But advertisers were buying in bulk and, in effect, were paying the same price for all impressions in a given bundle and all members of those audiences.

"To put it bluntly, there is money in inefficiency," says Mark Zagorski, the CEO of eXelate, a major data vendor. "The fuzziness of nonaccurate targeting is great for media owners [publishers]. [They] don't want to sell just the audience that advertisers want, they want to sell all the audience they can."

Using real-time bidding, advertisers can, if they choose to do so, use data to target individual prospective customers rather than just buying run-of-site impressions at sites where such customers are expected to browse.

"A carmaker might well be willing to spend one amount targeting a man browsing 'family cars' online, and far more on someone they believe is much closer to actually buying—perhaps someone they know has already booked a test drive, looked at different specs on a specific model, and priced insurance for it," says analyst Jo Bowman in an industry publication.[1]

RTB Enhances Strategic Targeting

The selection process involved in developing strategies for their real-time bidding encourages and enables advertisers to fine-tune the value they assign to individual customers. With real-time bidding, advertisers don't have to guess when they develop valuations for audience members.

"[Real-time bidding] enables the buyer to more precisely value what they're buying," says Tim Cadogan, the CEO of OpenX, an online exchange operator. "With real-time bidding you can bid what the impression is really worth to you."

That's two "enables" in two paragraphs. So how do advertisers learn more *precisely* what a given audience member is worth to them? The answer to that question lies in the speed of the auctions, which encourages trial and error by making the process fast and easy. Trial and error, with repeated corrections, produces the precision.

Here's an example. Suppose that the value of certain impressions is tough to gauge at the outset. Advertisers can buy them at the price that wins in the auction (which may be too high, too low, or just right—who knows?). Once they advertise to individual users, they soon see how these users respond to that particular ad. If some users don't offer a satisfactory return on investment, according to whatever metric the advertiser chooses, the advertiser can either bid less for the same or similar users or buy other users who seem more advantageous or cost less. Advertisers can repeat the process in an experimental way, even comparing a control group against a test group, and change their valuations of audience members based on real outcomes.

This quick feedback promotes rapid and continuing learning, assuming that the advertisers don't fall so in love with their initial media plan that they refuse to adapt it.[2] Advertisers can immediately see what is working and to which users it's most advantageous to present their ads. In this way they can quickly improve their targeting, the media they buy, and the creativity of their ad content.

"The rule is to allocate each media dollar where it works the hardest," says Kevin Lee,[3] the CEO of Didit.com, a search-engine-marketing consulting company. "Digital marketing is not a set-and-forget process."[4]

A prime benefit of buying online media by real-time bidding is that it can be prolific with insights about what is working—in the moment. As a result, media auctions using real-time bidding have been shown to be outstandingly effective. Here are the results of some studies:

→ Late in 2010, four of the major demand-side platforms determined that real-time bidding outperformed traditional run-of-network media buying methods by an average of 749 percent.

→ In a comparison of Google AdExchange campaigns running in April and May of 2011 executed by means of RTB vs. those executed by non-RTB mechanisms, RTB provided for a 19 percent savings on CPM rates and raised click-through-rate performance by 0.06 percentage points, from 0.09 percent to 0.15 percent CTR.[5] (A CTR of 0.1 percent—that is, a click by one out of every thousand users viewing a web page and taking action—is considered a respectable result. A 0.6 percentage point improvement in CTR is a more than 50 percent improvement in this case.)

→ Even more important, based on metrics set by advertisers, media bought by RTB by four big DSPs provided double the return on investment compared to non-RTB campaigns.[6]

RTB Display Ads vs. Paid-Search Advertising

For years, display advertising has offered the promise of superiority to paid-search advertising. It offers the means for far more creativity than a placement or link on a search engine results page (SERP). When well-crafted, display ads can be more immersive. They lend themselves to rich media options, such as expanding windows, animation, and full-motion video.

In addition, display ads can amplify the creativity and effectiveness of your sales pitch. For example, suppose you are a luxury carmaker—say, BMW. By using data adroitly, you can send your enticing BMW pitch to Internet users whom you have identified as recent Lexus searchers or Lexus website browsers. This technique is called search retargeting or site retargeting. This use of retargeting can endow display advertising with the same intent that has been touted as a key selling point in search advertising.

Yet display ads sell for cheaper prices than paid-search ads. Advertisers place a higher value on search ads because search engine users are thought to be more focused, attentive, intent, and disposed to act. They go to a search site to learn about something, as opposed to being passive perceivers of whatever display ad flashes before their nonintent eyeballs to stimulate their sluggish and nonmotivated neurons. At least, that's the caricature of how the two sorts of ads are presumed to function.

Because of the supposed greater intent on the part of audience members who use search engines, paid-search advertising has outsold display advertising since 2003 (around the inception of RTB and still today). Nevertheless, paid search has drawbacks when compared with display advertising. Search terms that get high click-through rates sell for high prices, as much as $25 per click. In addition, on the SERP there are only a few positions that are worth a lot of money because only the top three or four usually are clicked on. Then, too, SERP ads are less attractive, generally consisting of lines of text, text ads, or links—the least engaging, least immersive, and weakest brand-building ads. Perhaps most important for branding, Internet browsers spend only around 5 percent of their time online at search engines. They spend 95 percent of their time online elsewhere. Search engine users may be focused intently, but they are present only briefly.

RTB and the Growth of Display Advertising

Since 2010, exchanges offering real-time bidding for display ads have arrived, overcome advertisers' initial inertial resistance, and gained strong momentum. "Back in 2010 real-time bidding for display ads was more a concept than a reality for many," says Tim Cadogan, whose firm, OpenX, operates an online exchange that started offering RTB early in 2009. "Now it has become a mainstream reality. RTB has scaled and everyone is taking this space very seriously."

Powered in part by the increasing use of exchanges for selling display ad space using real-time bidding, display advertising is now growing significantly faster than search. In 2012, search grew 14.8 percent compared to the year before; display grew 19.9 percent. In 2013, search grew 14.9 percent; display grew 20.8 percent. An eMarketer forecast indicates that in 2014 display will grow an estimated 23.8 percent, leaving search far behind, with growth of 13.4 percent.[7]

However, it would be misleading to see this as a race between a tortoise and a hare. Actually, it's a race between two hares: paid search and display are two of the fastest-growing ad formats in the United States. (The only formats that have been growing faster are mobile and digital video, and those growth rates are in comparison to much smaller bases than either display or paid search ads have.)[8] Real-time bidding for display advertising is a steadily growing new media sales method in online advertising. According to a June 2014 forecast by eMarketer, in 2014 $4.9 billion of digital display ad spending will be done by means of real-time bidding on online exchanges. That $4.9 billion represents around 22 percent of ad spending for digital display media. By 2018 real-time-bidded display ad spending will reach over $12.5 billion, almost 30 percent of all digital display ad spending.[9]

In 2013, sales of paid-search advertising amounted to $19.9 billion.[10] Sales of display advertising reached $17.84 billion.[11] Although it is still slightly behind search advertising in total annual sales, display advertising online is no longer the scrawny little sibling. As predicted by eMarketer, spending for display advertising will surpass spending for search in 2015.[12] By 2018, eMarketer predicts, search will be $32.1 billion, but display will hit $40.8 billion, one out of every two dollars spent for digital advertising, both online and mobile.[13]

When real-time bidding for online display ads began, the exchanges were used mainly for selling the remnant impressions that publishers couldn't sell themselves. "It was only the dregs," says Bill Demas, the CEO of Turn, "the lowest of the low." But RTB has become such an efficient way to sell media that the quality of the impressions going through online exchanges has quickly elevated. Although sales of digital display ads on online exchanges conducted by RTB constitute only 22 percent of all digital display ad sales,[14] "we know that is going to some number greater than 50 percent," says Demas. "Real-time bidding through online exchanges is far and away the leading phenomenon in online advertising."

However, macroeconomic statistics, such as the growth of annual sales, don't capture the experience of the change that real-time bidding is causing in practice. To get a sense of that, it helps to know what happens as it is being used in daily commerce. In Chapter 7, we'll pull back the curtain and see how this happens.

CHAPTER 7

How Real-Time Bidding Works

When an Internet user types the address of a web page in the address field of his or her browser and hits the Return key, advertisers are instantly alerted to the impending presence—and the momentary attention—of that user. Potential advertisers quickly find out the person's lifestyle, Internet browsing history, and shopping habits. An auction is held for the chance to present an ad to that user on that web page at that time. The winner of the auction presents its ad.

All of this takes place in less than two-tenths of a second—less time than it takes for the web page to show up on the user's computer screen. Everything goes on, unobtrusively, behind the scenes. Most Internet users are unaware of what's happening, even though they, and their evanescent attention, are the focus of all this activity. By the time the web page appears on the user's screen, the transaction for the media is finished and the ad is in place.

Several commentators have said that real-time bidding for online media is like the New York Stock Exchange. But the analogy is only partly accurate.

What the stock exchange and online auctions do have in common is that bidding occurs and someone gets something, which they have to pay for. At the stock exchange they get shares of stock at a price the seller accepts. In an online auction advertisers get the right to present an ad on a web page to a certain Internet user at that time at a bid acceptable to the seller, the publisher of the website.

Like the stock exchange, online exchanges collect inventory (ad spaces, or impressions, on web pages) and corral trading into one hub. Imagine how inconvenient it would be if you had to go to one stock exchange to buy airline stocks and another to buy shares of carmakers. There was a time when the online display ad business was like that—a legacy of the print and old-media ad networks, many of which were set up to sell ad spaces in narrowly defined categories. As a result, an advertiser often had to go to more than one ad network to select media, which could be quite a hassle. That changed with the advent of online ad exchanges. Now advertisers can go to one exchange and bid for ad spaces from many sites.

One big difference between the stock exchange and an online ad exchange is the life span of the merchandise. On the stock exchange the shares of various companies exist both before and after the stock trade, whereas in online display advertising the impression exists only when a given user goes to a particular Internet address and sees it. The momentary behavior of the Internet user—the act of turning his or her attention to a web page that shortly will appear on screen—is what creates both the occasion for the advertising and the ad impression itself. When the user clicks on the ad, he or she is responding by means of the very media that presented the ad.

Every time an impression is auctioned using real-time bidding, there comes a moment when someone, a demand-side platform or an ad agency's trading desk, must decide whether and how much to bid. Their automated systems have been alerted that a particular impression is for sale on an online exchange, and they can either respond or not. That moment when bids are asked for is called a *bid request* or, sometimes, a *query*. In the world of online auctions, a bid request is the same as an auctioneer asking the audience for a bid on an object.

"Think of it as a jump ball," says Ramsey McGrory, formerly the head of Right Media (now owned by Yahoo!).[1] "Only online it's happening faster than the blink of an eye."

The growth of these bid requests is speeding up dramatically. In January 2011, Turn reached an all-time record of 100,000 ad queries per second going through its bid decision system. "[As of April 2014,] we are now seeing as many as 1.3 million ad impressions per second," says Bill Demas, "a tenfold increase in our real-time-bidded throughput in three years."

That's like identifying, putting a value on, and bidding for every drop of water going over Niagara Falls every second. And that's at just one firm.

It sounds amazing, and it is. The auction, the ad placement, and the appearance of the web page on the user's screen all happen in a few thousandths of a second. A complex process happens so effortlessly and so invisibly that it blurs the line between technology and magic.

Indeed, when you consider what's happening, real-time bidding does raise some questions:

→ How does the process know *who* is going to a web page?

→ How can an advertiser decide so quickly how much it is worth to show an ad to that person? The advertiser has no clue—in advance—that a certain user will go to a certain web page. It's not like placing an ad on a popular mass-audience TV sitcom, where the demographics are known.

→ How can the advertiser make a decision about how much to bid?

→ How can the exchange conduct an auction and determine who wins the auction so fast?

The Mechanics Behind the Magic of RTB

To understand it better, let's go behind the scenes and see how it works, step-by-step.

1. Suppose you're running your Internet browsing application program (browser). In the blank address field you type the address (the URL) of the Internet page that you want to see. I work at Hearst, a publisher, so I'll assume you want to see a page at one of our sites: www.cosmopolitan.com.

2. As soon as you hit the Enter key, the browser sends a request for the web page you want to Hearst's computer (our server), the one that hosts our website. The page you requested is a part of that site. This request is called a *get request* and it is made in HTML code.

3. Our computer, along with the computer systems of a multitude of our suppliers, sends editorial-content-related code back to your computer so that it can reproduce the web page you want. This code will give you the text, images, and other editorial content of the page as well as information about the formatting of that content.

4. In addition, our server sends your computer some other code called an *ad tag*. This code pertains to the ads that could be on the page you requested. When this ad-related code in JavaScript reaches your computer, it self-executes and alerts the ad exchange. This subsequent request from our server via your browser that is sent to an exchange, which is called an *ad call*, asks for advertising for the blank spaces on the page (the impressions).

5. Getting the ad call tells the exchange that it has a chance to conduct an auction and serve ads on the page you're going to see. The ad call also gives the exchange access to you.

How does our server know anything about you? When you come to our site for the first time, we send back to your computer a bit of code, called a *cookie*. It's a string of text. Figure 7–1 is a picture of such a cookie.[2] As an identifier, it's arbitrary and cryptic. The text of the cookie in no way characterizes you. It has as little to do with you as the license plate on your car or your phone number. However, if you come to our site again, we retrieve the cookie we placed on your computer the first time you visited us. That allows us to recognize you as someone who has visited our site before.

On that second visit, we send back another cookie. Cookies are always short strings of code, no more than 256 characters. By using them, we can keep a log of the user's visits to our site, which we amplify with each subsequent visit. That log exists on our computer. The cookies we place and retrieve are completely anonymous. There is no personally identifiable information connected with them. It's as if you were anonymously attending a conference we hosted, and the name tag you were wearing was blank. We wouldn't know specifically who you were, but we could tell, say, from the color and the pattern of the border around the badge, that you were attending the conference as a guest of Hearst Corporation. That's just what placing a cookie on your computer does. Moreover, you are free to erase the cookies if you wish. (Chapter 11 discusses this in more detail.)

6. The exchange now has the ability to read its cookies on your computer. (Let's assume that you've gone to the Internet before and seen pages with ads that resulted from auctions conducted on the exchange.)

```
ad-id=A6Y69bSbwU-yo968C00-LwI; ad-privacy=1
```

FIGURE 7-1   *The code shown here is a browser cookie placed on the computer of a visitor to a Hearst web page.*

7. When the exchange previously conducted auctions and served ads to your computer, it placed a cookie on your computer.

8. The exchange finds the cookie it placed on your computer, which allows the exchange to recognize you as someone who has seen ads that it served.

9. On its computer the exchange has a different, unique, coded identifier for you. These identifiers are encrypted. Let's say the exchange's code for you is ABCD. Again, these bits of code referring to you are just strings of code, not your name or any other personal identifier.

10. The exchange sends your coded identifier to all the advertisers, DSPs, ad networks, and others that participate in ad auctions on the exchange. The code alerts them that there is an opportunity to send an ad to a user (you) that the exchange calls ABCD. It informs them that an auction will take place.

11. When the exchange sends the ad call to the companies that participate in its auctions, it enables those companies to find any cookies they might have placed on your computer when they participated in previous auctions, won them, and presented ads to you.

12. In addition, the prospective bidders make use of other, non-auction-related opportunities to place cookies on your browser. For example, if it's an advertiser, you may have gone to that website and registered on it, and when you did, the advertiser placed a cookie on your computer. Each of the potential parties to the auction finds out what they know about you by retrieving their cookies from your computer and looking up your record in their respective databases. That record shows when and how frequently they have advertised to you in the past, along with information about the types of sites you have visited, which they can determine based on where those earlier ads appeared.

Each of the advertisers (or, more likely, the firms working for them, such as their DSPs, ad networks, and ad agencies) has developed a profile about your online browsing and what ads you've seen. For example, in this file they may note that you've seen ads for Toyotas when you went to Toyota's website, ads for diapers when at the Procter & Gamble (P&G) website, or ads for Fidelity when at Forbes.com. They don't know your name, but they know a lot about your browsing and buying habits, and they are always enlarging the profile they keep about you.

They have been able to amass this profile because their ad agency or their DSP has participated in auctions on behalf of clients such as Toyota, P&G, or Fidelity. The profile they compile is associated with a coded identifier that they have set up for you. To the advertiser and/or its DSP, you are user 1234, who may have received ads from Toyota, P&G, or Fidelity.

They also know one final key thing: The user whom they know as 1234 is the same user whom the exchange identifies in code as ABCD. Because they know that 1234 and ABCD refer to the same user, they are able to connect all the dots. Making that connection is called *cookie matching* or *cookie syncing*.

13. All the DSPs (let's assume that it's the advertiser's DSP) that are considering participating in the auction do this cookie matching.

Because the exchange's cookie and the DSP's cookie refer to you uniquely, the DSP can use its profile about you to decide how much it will bid for the chance to serve an ad to you. Let's say that the profile shows that you've repeatedly browsed jewelry sites and that sixty-four times you purchased diamonds larger than 10 carats. That might convince the DSP that you're a good candidate for an ad for an executive jet, a multimillion-dollar piece of real estate, or an expensive cutthroat divorce attorney. They don't know whether your name is Trump or Berlusconi, but, just as the salesperson in the shoe store sizes you up by the quality of your shoes and whether they are shined, they have learned enough to give them (as the prosecutors say) "probable cause" to think you have high value as a viewer of ads for expensive merchandise and to pay plenty for you in the auction.

14. All advertisers set a value that they will bid for the right to show you their ad, and these bids go into the auction.

When the auction occurs, the computer at the exchange can scan for bids and see what every advertiser is willing to pay for you. This value–lookup function is like the computer at a stock exchange that sees what limit orders are on file from traders wanting to buy a particular stock. (A *limit order* is an instruction, say, from a broker, telling a trader or exchange that a particular buyer is willing to pay up to $X for a certain stock.) The same thing happens when you tell eBay what your maximum bid is.

15. An auction takes place in real time to win the right to put an ad on the page that is about to appear on your computer, and a winner is determined.

In most cases, auctions that take place online in real time are *Dutch* or *second-price* auctions (for more details, see Chapter 4), where all bidders immediately make their highest bid; no time is wasted on multiple rounds of bidding. Instead, resolving the auction and determining the final bid rankings is merely an exercise in number crunching, which the exchange's computer does with lightning speed.

16. The exchange notifies the winning bidder.

17. The winning bidder's ad server sends the code for the ad to your computer.

18. The ad appears at the same time as the web page is displayed on your computer.

Now that we have seen how real-time bidding works as fast and as efficiently as it does, in Chapter 8 I'll tell how one of the pioneering ad-serving systems was developed at an ad network called Right Media.

CHAPTER 8

Right Media Builds Its Ad Server

S uch high-speed wizardry wasn't even a glimmer of an idea for Brian O'Kelley when he went for a job interview at a start-up called Right Media in March 2003. O'Kelley, then 25, had been a computer science major at Princeton, doing research on distributed processing systems. He also had built some personalization technology for American Express.

At the time, Right Media was an ad network start-up consisting of Mike Walrath, the founder, and Matt Philips, his first hire. The two had met while working in DoubleClick's media division. Walrath and Philips were gypsies, a two-man team of yield-optimizing wannabes. Ad networks, then, were a scrappy business. With Right Media, Walrath and Philips were trying—for the third time—to chart their own course.

The Origin of an Idea

Walrath had been a salesperson at DoubleClick, buying impressions cheap and reselling them for a profit to major customers such as AOL, Match

.com, and Colonize. DoubleClick's media division then was one of the largest ad networks in terms of number of ads served—the McDonald's of ad networks. It had the world's largest ad-serving system, called DART, then a big and fast impression allocation platform. All the ads sold by salespeople were served by this platform.

Walrath was DoubleClick's most productive salesperson, at least when it came to selling performance-based media, meaning with results guarantees as measured by metrics such as cost per click, cost per acquisition, or click-through rate. DoubleClick was only his second job after graduating (as an English major) from the University of Richmond. His first job was as a personal fitness trainer. He moved up to become a manager and sold training services for New York Sports Clubs, a chain of health clubs.

Philips was also not a computer geek. He didn't write code. He wasn't a salesperson, either. His expertise was in straddling both the business and the techie sides of DoubleClick. He could talk to businesspeople and to techies, and he was adept at the back-and-forth translation between them. Officially, Philips was a product manager, but he also served as a liaison between the media division and the technology division.

At DoubleClick, Philips had been asked to analyze the feasibility of cost-per-action pricing (whereby the price would depend on the results, based on some measure of performance) and to determine whether the company's ad server could handle both the ad serving (placing each ad on the correct web page on behalf of the advertiser) and this alternative variable form of pricing.

At the time, DoubleClick's system was handling the ad serving for vast quantities of ads. Companies with systems set up to crunch huge numbers in one way are rarely receptive to monkeying around with their platforms to do things differently. This unwillingness often leads both customers and the company's salespeople to an exasperating, chicken-and-egg impasse. We don't support that because nobody is asking for it. But nobody is asking for it because you don't support it. And, although they had asked

Philips to investigate this form of pricing, they exhibited little interest in pursuing it.

DoubleClick's platform was essentially a gigantic dump truck. It filled and dumped and filled and dumped. The ads were served in real time; that is, they appeared in the correct spot just as the web page showed up on a user's computer screen. But the other functions, such as performance assessment or billing, were tidied up later at a much slower pace. The platform was a prisoner of its own tunnel vision. It couldn't think in terms other than price. "It would look at all ad [spaces available] and saw only their [price] tags," says Philips. If you're a hammer, everything tends to look like a nail.

There really wasn't much interest at DoubleClick in thinking about how to make the most of the system or how to make more money by using it differently. Getting revenues in other ways wasn't given much consideration. "We were selling shovels," says Philips, "not mining gold." Then again, "I was asked what the market wanted," he says.

He introduced himself to Walrath. They went into a small conference room. Behind closed doors, they conjectured and they quarreled about how ad serving could be done better. Both of them wanted the ad-serving system to be smarter in terms of pricing and the revenues that could be expected depending on which ad was shown to which user.

Because he sold impressions with performance guarantees, Walrath wanted to change DoubleClick's ad-serving system so it would select the impressions that would perform best. No matter what metric the advertiser wished to use to measure performance, the ad media bought had to meet the advertiser's performance objectives.

Every day Walrath would get a spreadsheet printout that showed which ads on which sites were performing well or poorly. Every day Walrath was faced with the chore of reviewing the spreadsheets and deciding which impressions from which sites were not performing well. He would then manually remove those sites from his customers' campaigns to optimize their performance.

Walrath wanted to automate this optimization process. He was sure that some algorithm could cull sites with low-performing impressions and save him from having to manually perform the laborious process every day. Automating this process was the main aspect of Walrath's vision, at least initially.

A few days after their first meeting, Walrath and Philips had that "Jesus in the trees" look in their eyes—a vision of what a responsive, flexible, ad-serving system could do. Now they had to sell it to DoubleClick.

Few at DoubleClick really understood Walrath's and Philips's vision for an enhanced ad-serving system. Walrath doesn't claim he was much of a visionary. "All I wanted to do was automate the work I'd been doing manually," he says. Yet, if one definition of a visionary is someone who understands something more deeply than the people around them, by that definition Walrath was a visionary. "It was visionary enough that the people at DoubleClick laughed me out of the room," he says. "Most people who do something that disrupts, they do it from within the system that is not performing well. You have to understand how it's broken to think of how to build it better."

Some at DoubleClick did get it. Nevertheless, they told Walrath and Philips to forget about it because DoubleClick was trying to sell off the media division. It was the post-9/11 period, a time of severe belt-tightening at DoubleClick. Media buys from brand advertisers were drying up. The online advertising market as a whole was experiencing a gigantic over-hang. There was a huge oversupply of media, and demand was dwindling. Sometimes 30 percent or more of DoubleClick's inventory went unsold. The glut of media was driving down prices (CPMs).

The little subsection of DoubleClick's media division that sold impressions on a pay-for-performance basis was called Sonar. It was the only part of DoubleClick's media division that was profitable. It had twenty-three salespeople, one of whom accounted for 40 percent of the sales of the entire media division. That salesperson was Mike Walrath. Bill Wise, now CEO of Mediaocean, a company providing a digital media platform for advertisers, had started Sonar and was then running the media division. "DoubleClick's media business was losing a ton of money," he says. Sonar was the one bright spot.

One day Kevin Ryan, then the CEO of DoubleClick, asked Wise who Walrath was. "Trust me," Wise replied, "someday we'll both be working for that guy."

For Walrath and Philips the question was: Whom would they be working for tomorrow? "DoubleClick had this big monolithic dinosaur that all their advertisers were plugged into," says Philips. "So they wouldn't have gone for our vision even if they weren't going to sell off the media division."

Seven months later DoubleClick's media division was sold to L90, another ad network (its name was later changed to Max Worldwide). Wise, Philips, and Walrath were shipped off to L90. When Walrath and Philips started lobbying there for the development of their new system, they were again told to forget about it. Why? Because L90 soon was going to be acquired by Excite, which had an ad server that it was going to continue to use.

Walrath and Philips were thwarted for the second time.

Finally, Walrath had enough. "This can be done," he told Wise. "I know it can be done. I'm going to go somewhere and do this."

He then met with Jonah and Noah Goodhart, brothers who, in 1999, while in college, had started a marketing agency called Colonize, funding it with money borrowed on their credit cards. It had grown to the point where they were spending millions of dollars with Walrath and had become one of his largest clients at DoubleClick.

The Goodharts realized that if the firm (which Walrath planned to call Right Media) was successful at automated optimization, it could threaten their business. They also realized that it offered a lot of opportunity and that Walrath had the right experience to do it. So when Walrath asked them to invest in the new company, the Goodharts agreed to invest $250,000 and become the new business's first client. Walrath and Philips defected, and in 2003 Right Media was born.

Growing Pains

The CEO of Poindexter Systems,[1] Joe Zawadzki (now CEO of MediaMath, a DSP), let Walrath and Philips run Right Media in the little back room in Poindexter's office. The room, formerly a supply closet, had no window. Only four desks could be squeezed into it. The rent was $500 a month.

This palatial setting was where Brian O'Kelley had his job interview. When he arrived, O'Kelley was intrigued about how to automate optimization processes. "I had expertise in real-time prediction, personalization, and delivery," says O'Kelley, "but my academic background is in scalability."

Unfortunately, O'Kelley says, he did a bad job of scaling his salary requirements. He told Philips, who was vice president of technology, that he wanted $90,000 a year to start. At the time, Right Media was making good money. Within five months of starting, even though its visionary new ad server was still on the drawing board, it was booking more than $1 million a month with advertisers such as the Goodharts. Nevertheless, O'Kelley says, his salary expectations were over the top. He was rejected in real time. However, Philips suggested that he try to get a job at Poindexter.

Zawadzki took him on. "We hired O'Kelley to add capabilities to 'SmartServe,' an ad server that we had," says Zawadzki. "He was just a developer, but he turned out to be very talented." Poindexter was then a media optimization firm, helping ad agencies get the most out of their campaigns. It scored impressions and cherry-picked the ones that seemed advantageous for clients.

As Poindexter and Right Media grew, their personnel worked in each other's midst in the grubby loftlike space, the desks of one firm's employees among the desks of the other. It could be hard, in the forced intimacy of this ghetto of techies, to tell who worked for which company.

Soon the distinction became irrelevant. Walrath and Zawadzki agreed to start a joint venture. Poindexter pledged to amp up SmartServe, its ad server, and Right Media decided that, instead of developing its own server, it would use Poindexter's. At the time, all Right Media had was a sheet of specifications—what the ad server was supposed to do. It trusted Poindexter to deliver a working system.

"We were agnostic about what system to use," says Walrath, "as long as it enabled us [algorithmically] to do the optimization." In return, Right Media would serve the ads for Poindexter's clients such as AOL. "Someone was going to get paid to buy that media," says Walrath, "and it might as well have been us."

Eleven years later, Philips says that this arrangement with Poindexter, not money, was why he rejected O'Kelley. He maintains that Right Media could have paid O'Kelley what he had asked for, but that, at around the time O'Kelley showed up, Philips and Walrath expected Poindexter to do the heavy lifting in the development of a state-of-the-art ad-serving system. Philips's plan was to hire someone to design only the user interface of the system, the front end. For that, he thought, O'Kelley was overqualified.

"I thought all we needed was a rowboat," he says. "Brian O'Kelley is a nuclear-powered aircraft carrier." That, he says, is why O'Kelley didn't get the job at Right Media and went to Poindexter instead.

At Poindexter, O'Kelley spent a few months poking and prodding its system, trying to understand its moving parts. "An ad server is a large-scale distributed system that predicts consumer behavior and makes decisions based on it," says O'Kelley. That is, if the ad server works. O'Kelley knew that Poindexter's did not work.

The Poindexter system (SmartServe) was real-time in that it could serve ads in a timely way to fulfill every ad request. In addition, it could cherry-pick impressions, meaning that it could pick the best impressions for a given advertiser. It also could do creative optimization, meaning that it could pick the best ads to show to a given user.

SmartServe wasn't designed to be a tool for an ad network. "The technology wouldn't enable you to manage multiple advertisers across a network of publishers," says Ted Shergalis, a cofounder of Poindexter. "[SmartServe] couldn't pick the right ad to maximize the revenues for an ad network," he says. In some cases, the system might serve the ad that would maximize revenues for the ad network as a whole, but in lots of other cases it wouldn't. Its primary aim—the problem it was built to solve—was serving the right ad for a given advertiser.

Moving On

Unexpectedly, the plug got pulled on the joint venture. Poindexter's board of directors, mostly venture capitalists, voted against approving the venture. They told Zawadzki to forget about it and just follow the strategy he had proposed when they had invested in the company.

To O'Kelley, this was a signal to reiterate his desire to work with Right Media. He met Walrath and Philips for lunch at a spot away from the office so that no one from Poindexter would see them together. He told them that Poindexter's system wouldn't do what they wanted it to do and that, because the board of directors had pulled the plug on the joint venture, Poindexter was not going to innovate any further.

Furthermore, he assured them that he could build the system for Right Media within six months. To back up his claim, he offered to work as a consultant and leave when he finished the project. Moreover, he said he would work without getting any equity in the venture. Finally, he emphasized that, if they didn't take him up on his offer, he was going to leave Poindexter anyway because there was no longer anything of interest for him to do there.

"Yeah, I was a mole," O'Kelley admits. "I had spent months [working] in the same space. I knew [Poindexter's] stuff didn't work. I told [Walrath and Philips], 'You can't use [Poindexter's system]. It doesn't work. I'll build you a better one.'"

Here was a guy whom Philips had turned down for a job less than five months before telling him that he and Walrath should bet their business on him. However, since then, circumstances had changed drastically, leaving Right Media with only itself to rely on to develop the ad server. "If we were trying to build this whole thing ourselves, then we needed to hire someone like [O'Kelley] with so much firepower," says Walrath. "If you want to go to war, you need more than a rowboat," adds Philips. "You need an aircraft carrier."

Even though O'Kelley was willing to work as a consultant, without equity, and offered to supply his own ejector seat, in August 2003, Walrath and Philips hired him as a salaried employee of Right Media.

Two months later, O'Kelley and Philips demonstrated a working prototype to Walrath. He didn't like it, dashing the high hopes they all had. Walrath says that the system didn't have the business logic to understand the nuances of the ad network business, the needs that he, as a salesperson, lived with every day and deeply understood.

It was a day of brutal disappointment for all three, the kind of dreadful experience when the possibility that you could really fail suddenly seems shockingly likely and extremely demoralizing. Each left the office wondering if what they should be developing was a Plan B for their careers.

"It was a tough day," Walrath admits. "A big explosion. We had to start from scratch."

Walrath decided to work directly with O'Kelley. Fairly soon after, as development continued, O'Kelley became chief technology officer. "It became clear that [O'Kelley was] my boss," says Philips. "For the next four years I worked for him. The single most amazing thing I did in my four years at Right Media was to hire Brian, although it took me two tries."

One of the limitations of the DoubleClick ad server had been its tunnel vision. It tended to see everything in terms of CPMs and always gave priority to CPM deals. This led it at times to ignore pay-for-performance deals that might have been more lucrative.

By contrast—and this was a big difference—the system O'Kelley designed for Right Media had the capability to translate every potential deal into a common denominator called *effective CPM* (eCPM). The simple equation for the translation algorithm, developed by Philips, can be written as:

$$CPC \times CTR \times 1{,}000 = eCPM$$

CTR represents the click-through rate, which is the rate at which an ad converts (in this case, what percentage of users out of one thousand shown an ad clicked on it). This assumes CTR is the measure the advertiser wants to use to assess performance. But any other performance measure could be put into that spot in the equation.[2] CPC stands for cost per click. That spot in the equation can likewise be replaced with any kind of pay-for-performance pricing terms agreed upon when the deal was made. The result represents the revenue expected from a thousand ads based on how many users per thousand presentations clicked on them.

This conversion equation made the Right Media server a more flexible, responsive system. It could take any number of deals, convert them all to their respective eCPM value, compare them as "apples to apples," and then pick the deal whose impressions would make the most money for Right Media.

However, this assumes that the most advantageous deal could be predicted—that the system could foresee the click-through rate (or whatever measure of performance) that would be achieved. But the CTR in the equation could not be known in advance. How could an algorithm know in real time how many clicks would result from one thousand impressions that had not yet been served? So many variables affect click-through rate: the site on which the ad appears, time of day, geographic region, how often the ad is shown, and how persuasive the ad is, among other factors. How could so many factors be assessed and an outcome predicted?

The ability to predict eCPM based on so many factors was a major innovation of O'Kelley's system.

To achieve that, O'Kelley studied a multitude of math papers, finally coming across something called a *naïve Bayesian network*. This multidimensional network is naïve in that it treats all variables as if they were independent of one another and weighs each equally.[3] The system O'Kelley developed based on this idea was one of the things that made the Right Media ad server different.

Basically, the algorithm assesses the ad campaign to see what factors—

age, gender, where the user lives, how often the user has seen the ad, what sites the ads appear on, household income, and so on—most affected whether a user would click on an impression. It then searches the database, which is updated hourly, to find out how many clicks on similar impressions had been received from other users who embodied those attributes.

Based on the assumptions that (1) the future would resemble the past in these respects (a big "if") and (2) these factors were the key factors (another big "if") in determining users' behavior, it forecast a click–through rate that was the same as the one exhibited by similar users in prior campaigns that were substantially similar.

In the way it predicted, Right Media's system was less savvy than a good handicapper at a racetrack, because it weighed all variables equally. In the real world, as opposed to being inside a black box, that's rarely the case. In the course of most events, some factors turn out to be much more influential than others in producing a result.

In a sense, a naïve Bayesian algorithm is always rounding up the usual suspects: the folks that conventional wisdom suggests would look favorably on the ad. Such an algorithm fails to find atypical users, those who might respond far more strongly than anyone might have expected. Such potential users get left out of consideration, yet they can be an untapped gold mine. For example, younger women customarily are not targeted for ads for hearing aids. Nevertheless, as a result of a bit of inspired data mining and hunch playing, marketers discovered that surprisingly large numbers of younger women were the ones who bought hearing aids for elderly parents who were unwilling to buy hearing aids for themselves.

O'Kelley doesn't make big claims for the accuracy of the algorithm's predictions. "It wasn't too accurate," he says, "but it was a hell of a lot more accurate than the algorithms being used by others. They were using an abacus. I was bringing in a slow calculator. But it was accurate enough."

Although this was not flawless prediction, it was *satisficing*, a term coined by Herbert Simon. It was a result that was adequate enough to be useful in the circumstances—as in here on Planet Earth.

Armed with the click-through rates predicted this way, Right Media's in-development ad server, called Yield Manager, went through every ad campaign that Right Media had contracted to fulfill to determine which ones, if selected, would make the ad network the most money. In effect, Yield Manager was holding an internal auction, and the expected eCPM the algorithm calculated for each campaign was that campaign's bid for the impressions needed to fulfill it. The campaign that produced the biggest bucks—for Right Media—was fulfilled first, then the next most lucrative, then the next.

This approach not only enabled Right Media to fulfill the campaigns that would make it the most money—a big advance—but also allowed it to automate the optimization process, which had been Walrath's main objective. There were still problems, however.

Nonalgorithmic Hassles

Even though O'Kelley's new algorithm was chugging away, optimizing as it was supposed to, in the media market outside its black box, Right Media faced a pervasive market mismatch. The media sweet spot—those impressions that would produce high response rates to whatever the advertiser wanted and was measuring—were always few and never enough. They were also expensive for Right Media and, therefore, less profitable. On the other hand, poorer-performing impressions were always cheap and plentiful. They made up 50 percent of Right Media's inventory. Aaron Letscher, who, during this formative period, was a salesperson, Right Media's second hire, explains, "We were choking on that inventory."

In addition, the way the optimization technology worked made it hard to combine poor-performing impressions with well-performing impressions. Yield Manager was designed to get rid of poorer-performing impressions, not to use them. It removed the lower-performing websites from pay-for-performance campaigns. This was counterproductive to Right Media's pay-for-performance strategy, because the poorer-performing impressions on those sites could produce some useful clicks to help achieve a performance guarantee *if* they could be mixed with other, better-performing impressions.

Since Right Media never had enough of the higher-performing impressions, it wanted to use the massive numbers of lower-performing impressions it had in inventory. It shouldn't make any difference how Right Media got the clicks. Clicks are clicks, right? If the guaranteed performance was achieved, then Right Media had accomplished the terms of its pay-for-performance deal.

Advertisers, on the other hand, didn't view it that way and were often irritated if they discovered that some substantial share of their clicks came from cheap, low-performing impressions or nonpremium sites. Pay-for-performance advertisers presumed that they were paying a per-impression price (like a unit price)—one they thought was expensive. (This wasn't an unreasonable assumption. Pay-for-performance campaigns were always higher-priced than those without performance guarantees.) Even if they got their money's worth—that is, the promised performance—if they sensed that their campaigns were being fulfilled using these dirt-cheap impressions, they were aggravated.

Getting enough scale and avoiding wasting impressions were the two horns of Right Media's dilemma. Walrath, Letscher, and other top salespeople, such as Ramsey McGrory, knew that the solution was to scrap the fixed-price model for impression transactions and, instead, to buy and sell them based on how well they performed. "There was no direct correlation between price and value because we were locked into a fixed-price model," says Walrath. "Why can't we just value media appropriately, I wondered."

If impressions could be bought for a price commensurate with their performance, he thought, Right Media could then buy impressions for what they were worth. If that could be done, then price and value would be coupled and campaigns could be fulfilled in a rational way.

That would require Right Media to get impressions from publishers and fulfill campaigns for advertisers when there was no certain price for either beforehand. (As we saw in our discussion of paid-search auctions, there is no certainty about the outcome when prices are set by auctions.) Furthermore, it had to convince advertisers to allow it to use junk impressions when their campaigns had been using only the higher-performing ones. Easier said than done.

Actually, it wasn't easily said, either. Walrath and Ramsey McGrory, who, as head of sales, was more or less the apostle to the advertisers, couldn't very well go to them and say, "We'd like to fulfill your campaigns using a lot of crappy impressions. And we can't tell you how much we're going to charge you for them. But not to worry; we're not going to charge you very much. Trust us."

This lacks something as a sales pitch, wouldn't you say?

Instead, Walrath decided to experiment and began combining good- with poor-performing impressions as if he had the advertisers' permission to do so.

What if we broke up every campaign into a bunch of subcampaigns, he wondered, each aiming at different performance targets and using media bought at prices suitable for each subcampaign? Wouldn't the success of the campaign as a whole be boosted by deploying media in that selective, more sensible way?[4] Walrath and McGrory began using the ad server to run multitudes of such subcampaigns.

O'Kelley hit the roof. This wasn't the way the server was designed to run. In retrospect, Walrath says, "It was yet another pivotal moment that involved Brian and me screaming at each other."

Lucky for Right Media, the ad server had not read its owner's manual. It didn't realize that it wasn't supposed to work the way Walrath's hacking was making it work. O'Kelley's griping notwithstanding, the server could do what Walrath wanted, and it started to fulfill campaigns with greater efficiency and effectiveness. The cost of the media for each subcampaign began getting closer to the performance value of the impressions. Waste decreased.

"We had dramatically increased the number of campaigns overnight," says Walrath, "and it created very real technical issues that could have been avoided had we been a little less aggressive in our experimentations. However, most of the innovation seemed to come from breaking something. [When things broke,] it sure gave us an incentive to address the issue quickly."

The fulfillment of the many subcampaigns pointed Walrath to the next step: to analyze campaigns down to the level of the individual impression. With some further development, the server could do that, too.

"Brian could rock the technology," says Walrath. "He never said 'that can't be done.'" More numbers to crunch maybe, but Walrath would buy O'Kelley more servers. (Or he would have, except that his credit cards and those of O'Kelley and chief operating officer Christine Hunsicker were all maxed out because some expected venture financing had not materialized.)

Through the synergy of experimentation, quarreling, and robbing Visa to pay MasterCard, O'Kelley built what Walrath asked him to. The server had an algorithm that predicted correctly the value *of an individual impression* based on its attributes and the historical performance data for a given campaign. This was a massive leap forward and one of the three things that made the Right Media ad server different and better than others: (1) It could convert every campaign to a uniform eCPM value, (2) it could optimize automatically and mix impressions that performed differently, and (3) it could value individual impressions. This was another and crucial step toward real-time sales of individual display impressions.

Right Media's system, Yield Manager, could now correctly value individual impressions. For the first time, value and price were coupled. The system was fair and unbiased, in that a given impression could be claimed by the advertiser for whom it had the most value—value as determined by the advertiser (for the campaign it was running) that bid the most.[5]

"It really was magic," says Walrath. "We were building stuff that was disruptive and innovative and it worked. It was so cool. Finally I had a sandbox that I could play in."

Real-Time Bidding

From there, it was just a small mental step for Walrath to wonder why they should charge fixed prices at all. Why not just get media, fulfill campaigns, and bill the advertisers for whatever the media turned out to be worth?

To Walrath, this new approach was as easy as stepping off a low curb, at least conceptually. He called it *dynamic CPM* (dCPM). However, putting it into practice meant changing the way business customarily was done, which also meant butting up against a major ad network competitor, Advertising.com.

Ad.com had a very different sales approach. While Right Media and other ad networks bought impressions using a contingent, revenue-sharing model, in effect buying media on consignment, Ad.com paid publishers fixed prices. By comparison with revenue-sharing sales, Ad.com's approach was like an addictive drug for publishers. It bought the publishers' media for pennies on the dollar, for horrifyingly low prices—but it bought vast quantities. A publisher might bemoan the fact that, because of such a big, flat-rate ad network buy, prices for its media were being hammered down. On the other hand, Ad.com was handing them a check for millions of dollars annually. No matter what happened, the publishers knew they could unload that inventory (much of it remnant they couldn't sell otherwise) and be sure of getting a fat check from the ad network. Then they had cash in hand, and Ad.com had the burden of figuring out how to use that inventory.

In thinking about buying media in a new way—charging for it only after the auction—Walrath was expecting publishers to give up the security of getting that big check in advance and offloading a big bucket of risk. This was also a tough sell because it was not long after the dot-com bust and publishers were sitting on mountains of unsold media.

According to Ramsey McGrory, at the time, some online publishers, using their own sales forces, failed to sell up to 70 percent of their media. They had become dependent on ad networks like Ad.com to compensate (literally and figuratively) for their disappointing media sales. Now Right Media was asking them to kick their habit for the big ad network sales that had been so comfortingly ensured.

Let's say, for example, that you are a publisher and are considering whether or not to sell your impressions to Right Media. Ad.com offers you a check for millions of dollars.

The Ad.com value proposition: guaranteed revenue.

The Right Media value proposition: Share the risk, and we will pay you after we see what media of yours we can sell and at what price we can sell it.

{Guaranteed Revenue} vs. {Risk + Pay You Later}

Which would you choose?

Walrath and McGrory added a bit more nuance to their pitch: Because we will be partners and sharing revenues from media sales, everything will be transparent. Even with this enticement, Walrath knew that convincing publishers to change how they did business was an uphill battle.

Transparency had some appeal. Fixed-price ad networks like Ad.com were opaque about the prices they received for their inventory. They bought massive chunks of inventory at rock-bottom prices, recognizing that advertisers (their customers) would pay a substantial premium for the certainty of knowing that they would get sufficient scale (a big enough audience to whom to present their ad). That, Ad.com had. It could have been called Scale.com. It simply held an auction and kept all the profit. In an old-fashioned (meaning largely opaque) market, where no one has a real sense of the inherent value of the media, you could get away with that. Like a bookmaker, Ad.com knew what the advertiser was willing to pay and what the publisher was willing to take, and it would play the spread.

By contrast, because he was always struggling to achieve scale, Walrath told publishers and advertisers a story about partnership, about prices and costs commensurate with the value of the media, and about openness.

Dealing with advertisers was an even harder sell. With dynamic CPM, Walrath was asking advertisers and agencies to give up fixed-price contracts for fulfilling their campaigns and give him complete autonomy to decide how much to charge them for an impression. "In effect they were writing us a blank check and we were filling in the amount for every impression," says Walrath. This was a gigantic psychic stretch for a lot of Walrath's customers.

One of the biggest advertisers at the time for both Right Media and Ad.com was AOL. It had been working closely with Poindexter before Right Media was launched. AOL was using online advertising to acquire new customers for its Internet access service. It was a lot cheaper to advertise online than by direct-mailing new-subscriber pitch letters along with disks of the software to use the service. However, 30 percent of the Internet traffic coming to AOL's site from click-throughs were from AOL customers. So 30 percent of AOL's online ad buy was wasted because it reached those who were already members.

After Right Media started, it began providing media for AOL on behalf of itself and Poindexter. Beth Wallace, who was vice president of online marketing at AOL then, worked with Walrath and McGrory at Right Media as well as with John and Scott Ferber, who ran Ad.com. Both Right Media and Ad.com were battling for a greater share of AOL's business. Each was touting the benefits of its new ad-serving impression allocation engine under development.

Wallace actually preferred Poindexter. Its tool was optimizing for AOL. The technology told Poindexter which impressions to serve and what ad content to serve to those users. Wallace thought that Poindexter's technology was the best for those purposes. While Right Media and Ad.com were working to improve the performance of AOL's ads, Wallace felt that the two ad networks were interested mainly in optimizing their own revenues. Poindexter, she believed, was the one most concerned with her business. "Joe Z[awadzki] had become in effect my business partner," she says. "He seemed the most invested in my success."

But Poindexter wasn't selling media; it was operating an optimization tool—a selection tool. For delivering media, AOL needed Right Media or Ad.com, or both.

Wallace wanted to know about the variables being used in each of their models. "I wanted to know more about the models because it helped me learn more about my customers and what worked with them," she explained.

Ad.com wasn't willing to let Wallace peek behind the curtain. "One of my frustrations was that they wouldn't be transparent about the variables of the model and how it worked," Wallace says.

She found Walrath and Right Media easier to deal with. "What made them successful," she says, "is that they partnered with us." Among other concessions, Walrath was willing to accept "passbacks." In other words, he agreed to allow AOL to return impressions that were not working well. This was the digital advertising analog of a used car dealer taking back a lemon and giving the customer a refund. Clearly, Walrath was willing to do whatever it took for a customer like AOL. Walrath also had an edge, Wallace says: "His tool was actually working."

So, at a critical moment in the start-up saga of Right Media, Wallace wrote Right Media a check for $5 million to buy impressions.

Right Media also had luck enlisting other ad networks as customers. One of its earliest ad network customers was a then-tiny firm called CPX Interactive. When Aaron Letscher made a cold call to CPX's "world headquarters" in Rockville Center, New York, he found a single room only slightly less grubby than Right Media's back room at Poindexter. It was 500 square feet, tops, but it had a window. Inside were five guys, all of whom would be asked for proof of age at a bar, and a big-screen TV. The five were watching *Judge Judy* when Letscher arrived.

However, when the head of CPX, Mike Seiman, turned his attention from Judge Judy's tongue-lashing some hapless defendant, he got what Right Media was doing. At the time, unbeknownst to Letscher, Seiman was about a quarter of the way along in developing his own ad server. When he learned that Right Media already had a working system, he realized that he could use it and save three-quarters of his projected development costs. In addition, he wouldn't have to harvest his media inventory all by himself. He could piggyback on Right Media's—use what it had without any publisher development effort, insertion orders, campaign monitoring, and expense for ad ops. CPX decided to test-drive campaigns using Right Media.

"CPX was one of, if not *the*, first to get how to use this," says Letscher. "The advertisers who were direct marketers, or who were the closest to being direct marketers, the ones who lived in the numbers, were the ones who tended to get this. Essentially, [CPX] was a direct response marketer and they were willing to take a risk."

CPX was soon joined by Oridian, another ad network. Right Media began signing up other publishers with mountains of unused, slowly composting inventory such as Tickle.com and MySpace.com.

The dynamic CPM pricing regimen was a big step forward, in that it coupled price and value, as determined by advertisers. Right Media's server had an algorithm that predicted the value *of an individual impression* based on its attributes and the historical performance data for a given campaign. Today, such sophisticated servers are as common as bonnets at an Amish barbeque. Right Media got a patent for its system. But there was one last leap to make.

What would happen if someone else—the advertiser, its agency, or its DSP—had the historical performance data but didn't want to hand it over to Right Media to work with? What about the advertisers who wanted to run data-informed, real-time bidding for impressions but wouldn't share their data or bidding parameters? Ever accommodating, Walrath agreed to allow them to plug into Right Media's ad server as a hub for buying impressions while they retained in-house their own impression valuation engine. As more advertisers and their agents did that, Right Media's ad server became an online ad exchange.

CHAPTER 9

Real-Time Bidding in Action

To understand why real-time bidding is such a game changer, we need to compare RTB to the way online media sales usually are conducted. Typically, the media selling and the ad operations behind the Internet's ad-serving process are planned far in advance. Scores of people sit in planning meetings for weeks before an actual ad is presented during a website's page-load process.

Making an ad placement without real-time bidding involves media planning, requests for proposals, contract negotiations, ad placements and tracking, and auditing and paying the intermediaries, each of which gets a cut. This process makes it more difficult to provide assurance that the ads actually get viewed by their intended viewers. As Mark Mannino, formerly vice president of self-service solutions at MediaMath, explains it, "[In 2006], to buy display online you had to call Forbes, you had to call Fortune, call everybody. It was a nightmare." That's because, until the advent of real-time bidding, there was substantial lead time between when the publisher declared its ad space for sale, when the advertiser announced how much it was willing to spend on a campaign, and when the ads were presented—too much lead time to be very effective, according to industry insiders.

"The biggest problem with [online] advertising was that decisions about what ads to show were made way in advance of when they actually appeared," says Brian O'Kelley, now the CEO of AppNexus, a major digital display ad–trading platform. "There are a lot of reasons you want to make those decisions as close to when the ads run as possible."[1]

Controlling the frequency of the impressions being served was another big concern that was the result of the traditional way online ad sales were transacted. When advertisers wanted large audiences and purchased ad space from a number of online publishers to amass the size of the audience they desired, they often could not control how many times their ad appeared, which led to waste and overspending.

Now auctions using real–time bidding on online exchanges have the potential to transform and disintermediate the intermediary–congested ad placement ecosystem and provide increased efficiency, reduced cost, and improved ad effectiveness.

Buy-Side Benefits

Let's look at some of the benefits that real–time bidding can offer advertisers.

Quickly Assess Potential User and Website

As we've seen, in every real–time auction advertisers (or their ad agencies, DSPs, or trading desks) conduct a split–second assessment of the advantages of showing an ad to a given user. Earlier we saw how, with real–time bidding, a carmaker can spend less for an online "tire kicker" and far more for a user who appears very close to making a purchase.

"Real-time bidding gives marketers the opportunity to look at hundreds of billions of impressions per month and only bid on those that are interesting to them," says Jeff Green, CEO and cofounder of The Trade Desk, a demand–side platform (Green was also cofounder of AdECN, the Internet advertising exchange acquired in 2007 by Microsoft).[2] The ability to browse with unprecedented scope and speed enhances advertisers' capacity to be selective about their ad spending.

Change Bids in a Flash

Because real–time bidding is dynamic, buyers can change their bids in an instant. Advertisers can also promptly learn what is working and change their ad buying, not just of an individual user but also across an entire campaign, based on real–world experimentation. Because RTB is so fast, it enables advertisers to pounce on opportunities as they occur. For example, they can shift to reach the target user at a different time of day if that seems to be working better.

Retarget to Enhance Effectiveness

With real–time bidding, an advertiser can *retarget* a user quickly to enhance the effectiveness of its campaign. RTB's speed makes it possible for an advertiser to buy impressions at sites known to be frequented by potential customers who are good prospects. This, in turn, helps the advertiser to quickly deploy its message so it appears soon after its initial viewing to those desirable viewers wherever and whenever they are browsing.

Cut Costs Through Selectivity

"Because every marketer can easily access so many impressions, display RTB remarketing is the lowest hanging fruit in all of online advertising," says Green.[3]

Not only does this gain in selectiveness improve effectiveness, it cuts costs. Advertisers can eliminate wasteful spending by no longer buying poorly targeted impressions. If a given user doesn't click or make a purchase, advertisers can remove their cookie from the retarget list. They can buy only the impressions that exactly fit their profile of the target customer. In addition, because exchanges get impressions from many sites, they offer advertisers many more sources for the customers they want and much less hassle aggregating them (one-stop shopping).

Granted, real-time bidding is not a guaranteed buy. An advertiser could find the perfect customer but lose the auction. But that customer can be easily tracked and found again, and the advertiser has the opportunity to sweeten its bid.

At the same time, real-time bidding offers the ultimate in transparency. It's the opposite of a blind buy. Advertisers know in advance exactly to whom they are presenting an ad and on exactly which site it will appear and at what time. This is a vast improvement over the often-obscure placements that were made using ad networks.

"Huge amounts of intelligence and data can be layered into this environment (more than any other marketing channel—on- or offline)," says Green.[4]

That means real-time bidding can offer a steady stream of insights to guide the decisions about which impressions to buy and to assess return on investment. "By learning what works for your campaign at the impression level, you have a great opportunity to identify trends and discover new insights about your best—and worst—consumers, context, and creative," says Mike Baker, the CEO of DataXu, a DSP. "These learnings can be used to guide strategy both within your campaign and across a broader marketing effort."[5]

Enhance Performance

The rapid learning that real-time bidding offers enables advertisers to adapt campaigns as they are running. Let's look at one aspect: how RTB helps advertisers increase the effectiveness of their ads' content. Since an advertiser can serve revised creative to some users and its original creative to others, this allows for great flexibility. With that in mind, suppose the original ad content works better with a subset of users; then serve them the original ad content. Suppose the revised ad content works better with other users. Serve the revised ad content to users *like those* in the group for whom it worked better. Advertisers can tailor their creative to the particular market segment to which they want to sell.

Real-time bidding can shed light on almost any variable considered in ad campaign management: time of day, geography, gender, age, frequency, and whatever other factor an advertiser chooses. All of these can be controlled with unprecedented finesse because advertisers are buying impressions individually. In addition, they have the ability to change their bids for each impression as the campaign evolves, to differentially value each potential user to whom the ad is shown. In the past, this information was never available quickly enough to make a difference.

Make Midcourse Corrections

For advertisers, the overall benefit of real-time bidding is better performance. With RTB, a campaign can become, in effect, a series of short-term trial runs. Each new approach can be a learning experience from which the advertiser can make sensible midcourse corrections. What had formerly been envisioned as a months-long campaign preceded by months of planning can now be an exercise in real-time dynamic adaptation.

Instead of being the marketing equivalent of a snowball rolling down the mountain, gaining mass and momentum, unstoppable and impossible to improve upon, campaigns can be fine-tuned through a series of useful adaptive changes in approach. It's likely that some aspects of any campaign will not work well, but, for practical purposes, a series of frequent, advisable midcourse corrections is indistinguishable from being on the right path.

Using real-time bidding this way is a good approach even if the advertiser's plans are indefinite at the beginning. Because they can be sensible about how much they pay for each individual impression, the cost of fine-tuning a campaign is not prohibitively high.

"Advertisers gain a much higher conversion rate through better targeting," writes Jo Bowman, an analyst at WARC, a British consulting firm.[6]

Bowman cites the example of a U.S. telecom company. It found that run-of-network ads bought using real-time bidding outperformed (as measured by orders received) ads acquired without the use of RTB by 562 percent and outperformed audience-targeted but non-RTB-purchased inventory by 44 percent.[7]

"Real-time bidding is hundreds and often thousands of percentage points more effective than display was [in 2008]," says Jeff Green. "Forget about every experience you had with display before because the world is different now."[8]

Improve Return on Investment

Another benefit of using real-time bidding is improved return on investment. Remember all of the toll charges along your journey from clicking on your browser to a fully loaded web page? They certainly won't disappear overnight—overhauling an industry takes time. But RTB has the potential to dramatically minimize the costs attributable to intermediaries and eliminate the redundant effort expended and paid for when many intermediaries mediate a process. Furthermore, the hidden transaction costs of doing business with separate yield optimizers, data shops, and networks can now be consolidated.

In addition to the savings achieved from the elimination of intermediaries, real-time bidding promises to bring about cheaper and more flexible pricing for ad impressions. With RTB, as each ad impression is bid on, an advertiser can specify what it's willing to pay. Real-time bidding enables advertisers to put a sensible value on each impression, stick to a budget, and buy only those impressions that they presume will pay off. They can pay for only those impressions they value most.

Maintain Greater Control

Real-time bidding facilitates buying individual impressions, which means greater control for advertisers. It provides advertisers certainty about what they're buying. Before being able to place real-time bids, advertisers were often put in the rather unprofessional situation of paying for something without knowing *exactly* what they were buying. Even with ad networks, advertisers had to place ads with a general range of sites and trust they would appear in the right places. Brands, or the agencies acting on their behalf, bought inventory in advance based on a reserved display space. They then had to wait to see whether execution matched their expectations.

The uncertainty created by buying in advance resulted in a double-blind experiment in which both parties could be disappointed with the ultimate implementation of a campaign. Because many advertisers didn't completely trust the process, they were disinclined to pay premium prices. By contrast, real-time bidding greatly minimizes the uncertainty of online media buying. With real-time bidding, advertisers can pursue precisely those impressions that deliver the greatest value for their brand. That can improve performance, however it is measured.

Gain Advantages for Branding

Real-time bidding is much more than a method for quickly assessing an impression's value and accomplishing a transaction, although that increase in efficiency is big progress. More important, RTB can be instrumental in refining the efficacy of online display advertising by enabling advertisers to learn much more about how to influence potential customers and how to assess their responsiveness to an ad campaign. To focus only on the transactional aspects of RTB is to miss a major advantage.

Real-time bidding enables marketers to better manage the subtle interactions that enhance brand awareness and influence the right customers for the brand. It allows brand marketers to purchase more specific groups of people and manage the interactions with them over longer periods. "Where real-time bidding comes into the picture," says Chris Stevens, vice president of Orbitz Worldwide, a travel site operator, "it allows the market to value users at some rational value based on their incremental influence, and value them less on coincidence, attribution error, and statistical illusions."

Over time, real-time bidding helps brand advertisers separate useful insights into the motivations of prospective customers from misleading metrics and illusory statistics. Focusing on a metric such as click-through rate uncritically can be misleading. "The Internet is basically a giant coincidence machine, and correlation often is confused with cause and effect," says Stevens. "The two are very commonly mistaken." Real-time bidding enables brand advertisers to develop statistical ways of factoring out such coincidence.

Real-time bidding also helps return scale to the system by congregating disaggregated individuals into groups whose movements can be tracked and who can be reached and targeted even though they are not and never will be together in any sense in time and space. By aggregating publishers from a multitude of domains, RTB once again allows advertisers to achieve scale—lots of tiny slivers but across a vast array of sites—with the added promise of precise targeting.

Sell-Side Benefits

Real-time bidding offers advantages for publishers—advantages that go beyond being able to sell remnant inventory. Auctions at online exchanges enable publishers to sell in an instant to a collection of advertisers that otherwise might not have been brought together. Although auctions can pit publishers against one another, as, for example, when the supply of impressions is much greater than the demand, the process can also work in the publishers' favor; for example, revenues can be boosted because advertisers are bidding against one another.

For impressions that have a clear value, such as affluent, in-market auto shoppers, the bidding can drive prices for such impressions higher. In the past, publishers often had to accept cut-rate offers from advertisers or from ad networks, which then resold the impression for higher prices later. Now, for such desirable users, the advertisers' need for scale can lead to prices being bid up. Publishers gain because advertisers will pay a premium for space that they know reaches the people they want. This would not have been possible when impressions were sold weeks in advance. Real-time auctions enable publishers to sell such desirable in-market auto shoppers *soon after* they were browsing cars online.

As Kyoo Kim, a former ad sales executive at MSNBC.com, noted, "We saw a real jump in unsold inventory submitted via real-time bidding platforms.... On individual ads, we've seen CPMs jump anywhere from 30 to 300 percent."[9]

That experience has not been unique to MSNBC. Tests conducted by PubMatic, a supply-side platform that serves the interests of publishers, showed strong improvements in CPMs. According to Rajeev Goel, a cofounder and the CEO of PubMatic, "In our early tests with select publishers and a dozen RTB buyers—roughly thousands of campaigns and billions of ad impressions—the impressions bought via RTB are monetized at CPM rates 60 percent (in some cases, more) higher than impressions not monetized via RTB."[10]

Real-time bidding also can give publishers a persuasive selling point for their media brand that competing search advertising cannot. For example, let's say an ad appearing on *Esquire*'s website is a strong influencer, but, right before making a purchase decision, the user does a Google search. Customarily, almost all of the credit for the sale is given to Google. Such presumptions ignore all the brand advertising and awareness creation that preceded the late-in-the-game Google search. "Giving Google credit for trillions of dollars in sales is like giving the checkout person in the supermarket credit for the sales of Kellogg's Corn Flakes," says Josh Shatkin-Margolis, formerly CEO of Magnetic, a retargeting company (now CEO of Purple Cloud, a retail communications company). Using RTB enables publishers to offer impressions when they would be advantageous for site retargeting, which contributes to advertisers knowing how the site influenced the eventual sale.

Benefits for Users

Are there any benefits for users? Yes. The more on-target ad serving offered by real-time bidding should provide users with ads that are more relevant to them, as well as fewer off-target ads whizzing past, less clutter, and less chance of "banner blindness." Not as big a potential benefit as may be realized by advertisers and publishers, the parties to the media buy, but a gain for users nevertheless.

Where Real-Time Bidding Is Headed

As a technology that has disrupted the established online media market status quo, real-time bidding has been criticized. Publishers have bemoaned the drop in prices they can charge and conflicts that can erupt in their sales channels. How can their salespeople keep charging premium prices when advertisers can buy impressions that seem the same for much lower prices in real-time auctions? In addition, buyers (advertisers) say that the impressions they bid for tend to be low quality. They are hungry for larger quantities of better inventory.

Despite such potshots by marketers and media buyers, who are, after all, the ones who authorize the ad spending, the surest sign of the viability of real-time bidding is that the heavyweight online market makers—Google, Yahoo!, and Microsoft—are behind it.

Google, especially, has thrown its weight behind real-time bidding and will probably do it more as sales of paid-search advertising slow. Perhaps in an effort to blunt criticism of the quality of inventory being sold by real-time bidding (some of it on AdX, the exchange it owns), on April 24, 2011, Google announced that it was selling "guaranteed premium inventory." This could have been a way for Google to get branding buys through reach and premium placements. If so, that would have been a new tack for Google. It prospered by emphasizing that it enables advertisers to serve the best ad based on the user's previous browsing behavior, relevance measures, and algorithms. Such an approach didn't always clinch the affinity of brand marketers.

"If they could combine the big spends that have historically gone to portals... with the efficiency and performance data that Google has become synonymous with, it's a big win for them," said Cathleen Ryan, then chief results officer of MEA Digital (now called Piston). "[Google] has spent a lot of time laying the groundwork, the 'pipe'..., collecting a ton of small and medium publishers that simply weren't big enough for networks to work with. Combined with premium, big destination sites, it's a whole bunch of reach, which, if you can guarantee [it] to advertisers, certainly competes with the biggest online publishers and premium networks."[11]

No doubt real-time bidding will face resistance from the toll collectors that don't want their positions as intermediaries eliminated. Yet buying display ads by using RTB offers efficiency improvements in media placements that are compellingly appealing. The speed of the systems will enable advertisers to reap such advantages with other media used on the fly, such as tablet computers and cell phones, as those markets mature.

Perhaps the surest evidence is the way the real-time bidding business has grown. In 2009, only 1 percent of all online display ads were bought on an RTB basis. In 2013, approximately 22 percent were sold by RTB, and that amount continues to grow as major publishers get comfortable with "programmatic sales" (automated selling by means of RTB).

As Triggit CEO Zach Coelius prophesied in mid-2010, "It is clear that a virtuous cycle is in full effect. At the end of the day real-time bidding and exchanges are simply more efficient markets, and looking back at the course of history, it is pretty clear that trying to fight against the market's drive to efficiency is always a pretty dumb idea."[12]

CHAPTER 10

The Impact of Data on Digital Advertising

Despite real-time bidding's ability to automate online auctions, send ads where they belong, and accelerate clearing operations, it doesn't work all by itself. However fast they crunch the numbers, algorithms don't have intuition with which to assess and sort impressions. Without the descriptive data associated with each of those zillions of ad spots, RTB wouldn't offer the advantages I've discussed in preceding chapters. In fact, it wouldn't work at all.

Stripped of its technological trappings, real-time bidding is a way of matching price with value. It enables nimble advertisers to quickly change the prices they bid if different impressions appear to have different values. But determining value comes first. This is important because in Dutch auctions, the type used by online ad exchanges in real-time sales of online media, there are no subsequent rounds of bidding during which prices can be raised. Data is the key to characterizing impressions, and characterizing impressions is the key to assessing their value. Without such data, bidding would be blind.

Data is also the key to finding useful impressions wherever they occur. Without it, advertisers couldn't find the users they need and bid to get them. It would be like trying to track a car without a license plate or a description of it. Before the advent of real-time bidding on online exchanges, advertisers had to depend on publishers to offer the right sort of users in large enough numbers in order to present their ads at the scale they required.

Real-time bidding has brought extreme speed to pricing, as well as automated sales and ad serving, but it has been data that has brought major increases in precision and individuation to ad targeting. Because of the data, for the first time in history advertisers can target individual consumers independently of their media choices.

"Data has become more valuable than the media itself," says Omar Tawakol, CEO of Blue Kai, a major data vendor.

What does that mean for *reach*, those to whom an ad is shown? Does it mean that finding the users is now a slam dunk?

Every decision about reach involves answering two crucial questions: "To whom?" and "Why?" These tacit questions have to be answered for every individual to whom an ad might be presented. Data is what makes those questions answerable and targeting warranted. It's the data guiding the ad serving that makes an ad suitable for the consumer to whom it is presented.

That's also what makes the advertising more effective. According to Dr. J. Howard Beales III, a management professor at George Washington University and former director of the Bureau of Consumer Protection at the Federal Trade Commission, behaviorally targeted advertising is more than twice as effective as nontargeted advertising.[1]

Data is the key—to value, reach, and effectiveness.

Data-Enabled Digital Advertising

The good news is that there is plenty of data. That's also the bad news. Every second, the data spawned by the behavior of Internet users grows exponentially.

As with the wake churned up by a speedboat, every time you interact with digital media by means of a networked device, you create, in effect, a wave of attributes that expands into an increasingly detailed characterization of yourself. The technologies of online advertising have enabled marketers and advertisers to juggle millions of impressions every second. Increasingly, each of those impressions is associated with an expanding constellation of data points—your attributes—that need to be considered and understood in order to be used advantageously.

In the early days of online advertising, data vendors such as Tacoda paid attention mostly to the web-surfing behavior of users. Selling razors to guys? Buy males by buying impressions on ESPN.com. Advertisers used browsing behavior as a proxy for users' dispositions, intentions, and engagement. Whether data confined to browsing behavior really enabled advertisers to know what to expect from a given user is questionable. But the aggregation of this rudimentary behavioral data had the effect of creating a passport of sorts. That enabled advertisers to find a user when he or she was online, and not just when the user was at the pages of publishers who happened to be selling the user as one of their audience members. This passport—an expanding ID profile—had the effect of diminishing the strength of the connection between users and the web pages they frequented and, therefore, weakened the proprietary rights that an Internet publisher could claim it had to those users.

Nowadays, advertisers and their data vendors harvest a greater variety of traits or behavioral aspects of users in order to learn how to target them and decide what media to buy.

With the proliferation of data comes specificity and precision in targeting a given user. While the content of the ad can't be custom tailored for each user, users—and their presumed responsiveness to an ad—can be selected with greater care. That improves the match between the ad content and those to whom it's presented. The better targeting improves the effectiveness of the advertising. Yet, as we saw when we looked behind the scenes at the operation of real-time bidding, all the players in online advertising have different data and different sets of attributes for specific users. They characterize each user differently because they are squinting at each user through different keyholes.

However, one of the consequences of collecting a lot of data for better awareness of prospective viewers is unprecedented complexity. All the complexity of creating and understanding the audience for an ad campaign has now gotten ratcheted down to the level of data. All the questions that concern online advertisers tend to pertain to data and how it should be used. Technology can help to handle the large number of attributes pertaining to users, but the questions about how to sort users and whether to show ads to this sort of user or that sort have to be answered thoughtfully. The marketing challenges remain the same, but they are playing out in decisions about what to do at a deeper level of information, where data is the differentiator. What to buy and what to pay for it remain key issues, whether the transaction occurs on an automated online auction exchange or by means of a sale negotiated by a salesperson. However, it's the data that represents and embodies the value that makes the media useful.

Two other and equally concern–worthy consequences of the increasing complexity and specificity of data are how big an audience can be aggregated and how fast that can happen. There is an inverse relationship between the specificity you can require for your target audience members and the size of the population that can be targeted.

The more specific your characterization of the user you want to reach, the more difficult it is to get a lot of them, even with the tidal wave of data being spawned. Suppose you wanted to advertise only to males over age 65 who are left–handed, wear trifocals, are tax–reform advocates, are vegan, and pack lunches for themselves but won't pack their sandwiches in plastic bags. Good luck finding a lot of them fast.

Marketers create profiles for their presumed ideal customers. These profiles tend to become more and more detailed and elaborate as marketers try to home in on the right candidates for their products. The data created by online advertising technologies now enables marketers to seek just the users with the combination of attributes they are specifying. Yet the more data–enabled that selection becomes, the more difficult it becomes to aggregate audiences that are big enough. Back in the early days of mass-audience TV advertising campaigns, marketers bought multi-million-viewer audiences, all of whom were watching *I Love Lucy* at the same time. Of course, each of those viewers was a unique individual. But advertisers treated them as interchangeable fungible sets of eyeballs.

Today, online advertisers are tending toward the other extreme. No customers are considered to be interchangeable once you get to know enough about them. Yet it becomes harder to get enough of them. Furthermore, they are probably most receptive to an ad at different times, certainly not all at the same time. (Remember, online advertisers are buying users individually and in the moment.)

Used unskillfully, data can swamp an online media buy and waste money. Used with finesse, data can create enormous impact.

CASE STUDY

Using Data Advantageously

At times, finding and using the right data works great. One aspect of the launch advertising by Universal Pictures for its film *The Adjustment Bureau* is an example of getting useful targeting by means of prospecting through massive data sets. The online ad campaign for the movie's premiere ran in January and February 2011. Universal's agency, Ignited, in El Segundo, California, spent much of its ad budget on conventional approaches: using a variety of contextual targeting (on sites frequented by movie buffs or those deciding what movies to see, such as Fandango.com and IMDB .com) and buying some premium content.

It also used demographic targeting. The movie featured Matt Damon, star of the Jason Bourne films. The preview made the movie seem a lot like a Jason Bourne thriller, showing Damon as a wannabe politician battling shadowy characters lurking in the background of his apparently conventional life. Men between 18 and 45 years old were expected to respond favorably. So Ignited bought that demographic group.

In addition, Ignited engaged DataXu, a demand-side platform based in Boston, to prospect for and optimize other useful impressions. It allocated only around 5 percent of its ad spend for the DataXu audience prospecting.

The campaign ran display ads offering a short version of the video preview of the movie. The measure of satisfactory performance was whether a user interacted ("engaged") with the ad. Engagement could mean clicking to watch the preview, listening to the sound track, or clicking through to the movie's website.

The campaign was brief and fault intolerant. Because it was going to run for just a few weeks before the film debuted, there would be no adjustment bureau for the advertising. If the targeting or tactics didn't work, there would be little chance to revamp the campaign by learning from mistakes.

"[Movie launches] have short marketing windows," says Dave Martin, the senior vice president of media at Ignited, "we don't have much opportunity to mine data to target the consumer. We didn't measure if we swayed peoples' intent. By the time you get the data the movie is already out."

DataXu began by analyzing impressions shown to users who interacted in one or more of the desired ways. For impressions that paid off (*converted*), DataXu analyzed the behavior trail and attributes of such worthwhile users (in the sense of being engaged with the ad in a way that the advertiser hoped) leading up to engagement with the ad. Then, using combinatorial optimization algorithms developed at MIT and used for NASA Mars missions,

DataXu developed a continuously improving predictive model of the users who converted.

Armed with this model, DataXu looked for users like those who paid off and held an internal auction to determine how much to pay for impressions to show to them. DataXu regularly looks at around 250 billion impressions each month on sixteen online exchanges such as Google's AdX as well as from Rubicon and Pub-Matic. DataXu's system evaluated and bid for hundreds of thousands of impressions every second while the campaign ran. All impressions were bought on online exchanges.

Of course, DataXu did not win every impression it bid for. Some were too expensive, given Universal Pictures' objectives. Nevertheless, it found plenty of users and discovered audiences that the movie studio and its agency hadn't expected to be significant.

For example, because the preview also showed an intense romance between Damon and Emily Blunt, as lovers struggling against the surreptitiously enforced confines of a predetermined fate, DataXu tried targeting women 18 to 49 years old. It got a strong response from that group. So it bought a lot more impressions targeting that demographic set.

Overall, DataXu's approach was to prospect for viewers by using a predictive model based solely on what worked. This was a sort of pragmatism that didn't care about stereotypical segments. The users to whom DataXu showed the ad could have been so different, one from another, that they might have been a completely random mix. No matter. If the ad worked with certain users, it worked. DataXu bought those users even if they did not fit into any predetermined audience category. The basis of its analysis and modeling was empirical observation rather than some marketing theory about groups of moviegoers.

Audience buying dominates advertising. Many advertisers and

their media buyers have customarily used an audience model developed by TV advertisers. But the Web often doesn't work that way. Recall the example I gave earlier about the hearing aids that were bought by the daughters of elderly hearing-impaired parents. If an audience marketer had bought only the elderly demographic group that it envisioned as users of the devices, it would have failed to target many potential purchasers.

"If you had gone out with a static media plan, you'd have been targeting the wrong audience," says Denise Vardakas-Styrna, a marketing programs manager at DataXu, referring to *The Adjustment Bureau* campaign. "You've got to be able to change directions on the fly."

There's no arguing with success. When the campaign was finished, DataXu had gotten more than twice the performance per dollar spent compared with the other audience or demographic buying methods Ignited used. Moreover, its online audience prospecting was the only aspect of the campaign that delivered such results at scale. It got fifteen times the reach the campaign's other combined approaches averaged. "[DataXu] achieved a lot from a cost-per-lift standpoint," says Dave Martin from Ignited. "It definitely exceeded our expectations."

Ignited would prefer to show prospective moviegoers a full-length (two- to three-minute), high-definition preview. A thirty-second version of the preview shown within a little banner ad on the web page is regarded as a shoddy alternative. "In a perfect world we wouldn't use banner inventory to sway someone's intent," says Martin. "But we don't live in a perfect world. The real world includes a lot of banners. From those banners we hope to get a reaction."

As with politics, this is "the art of the possible." Martin comments, "We have to buy banners and we have to get from banners what we [can]. But DataXu gave us a much better response from the banners they showed," meaning the impressions that DataXu bought happened to surpass the others at producing clicks.

DataXu's prospecting wasn't the only part of the campaign that made use of data. Every aspect of the online campaign made use of data.

The Adjustment Bureau received generally good reviews. Revenues were $21.2 million the weekend it opened, March 3–6, 2011. That was respectable, but not great for a movie that featured a big star like Damon. It came in second behind *Rango,* an animated parody of a western. *The Adjustment Bureau* campaign shows that how well data pays off depends on many factors. It is of instrumental value, and absolutely crucial for online auctions, but it is not the sole determinant of success. It is not, as the lawyers say, dispositive. Musical notes on the score of a symphony have meaning. They are data. Even better, the notes are the same at every performance. Yet not everyone gets the same results from playing them. It depends on how a given musician expresses those notes.

The same principle applies to making the most out of data about online users. Yet, by contrast with musical notes, data about online users changes constantly; these users are the proverbial moving target.

Online marketing has gone through a progression from buying media to buying audiences as proxies, then buying results in the form of clicks or whatever the chosen measure of effectiveness is. There is a gold mining aspect to data. You are always looking for those nuggets that work. How advantageously the data can be used depends on the skill of the marketers and on considerations that go beyond data.

"To make the best decisions in online advertising, marketers have to be able to score both the media and the data to determine how effectively they will accomplish the objectives that will be most useful for a brand," says Joe Zawadzki, CEO of MediaMath, a DSP.

As *The Adjustment Bureau* campaign also illustrates, using data for online advertising is about selectivity of the sort that lacks the opportunity for cultivation. There is always a happening-in-the-moment aspect to data. "You're never going to see that impression again," says Bill Simmons, the chief technology officer and co-founder of DataXu.

Then, too, an individual's responsiveness to ads changes constantly. Suppose an audience member could be identified with unerring precision, and that someone was the perfect subject to whom to show the ad. After seeing the ad more than once or twice, that person would no longer respond to it. This is known as *banner blindness,* and it is the reason that advertisers do not show an ad more than a few times (called a *frequency cap*). The takeaway: Even if the data selection is perfect, an audience cannot be kept on tap.

A person's responsiveness can also change because of changes in life stage. Suppose you learn that a given pair of users have suddenly become big buyers of diapers—clearly, they are new parents. At first glance, that may not seem relevant to an ad campaign. But often new parents are in the market for a different vehicle—say, a minivan—so they may now be a very receptive audience for a car ad online, whereas they hadn't been before. You've found a new reason to target them.

Data-enabled online ad serving is like catching a bird on the wing. Advertisers have to be ready to make the most of a fleeting opportunity. They also have to be ready to give up on it.

Marketers make a leap of faith that the data they are using is actually good. But a household can consist of a father, mother, son, and daughter—four very different people all accessed through the one computer. Whom do the cookies represent when the family shares the computer?

The Adjustment Bureau campaign is illustrative in another way. Its effectiveness depended on factors other than data. For example, its results were influenced by the decision to allocate only 5 percent of the budget to show banner ads to the users DataXu found. The low percentage allocated to DataXu's impressions may have diminished the overall effectiveness of the campaign. It might have been better to present many more banner ads, briefer and less appealing as they are, to that audience. Or perhaps the agency should have chosen a metric other than clicks.

All these issues were decided before DataXu was engaged. It had to work with the hand it was dealt. Important as data is, ad serving still is a subsystem that has to mesh with overall campaign management.

Even if a DSP or an ad agency had to deal with only the selection of data, buying effective online ad impressions would still be no cinch. Behind the scenes of this technologically enabled ad serving there are a host of decisive issues in finding, pricing, and delivering the ads.

There is another consideration about reach. Assuming you have the time to get the right users to present to, how can you be sure that you've got *all* those you want? Suppose you are a resort destination that advertises online. This aspect of reach translates into two issues: coverage and distribution. Coverage addresses the question, for example, "Did you get everybody who is interested in making a trip to Hawaii? Distribution concerns the issue of where to find them. How do you know where they go? Where can I find and correctly identify them?

Data's Plumbing Problems

For publishers, one of the key concerns is leakage. Is the data about valuable users seeping out or being scraped from publishers' sites, enabling advertisers to access those users somewhere else where impressions are cheaper? Some publishers worry that this leakage will decrease their sales.

Here's a hypothetical example. Let's suppose a user frequents Forbes.com, a site that charges premium prices for its users, its audience members. Now let's suppose that advertisers somehow get data off the Forbes.com site that enables them to identify those users when they are visiting a site whose impressions are much cheaper. They use real-time bidding to buy those cheaper impressions and don't buy the more expensive Forbes.com impressions. That cuts revenues for Forbes.com. Such data leakage is a big concern about the plumbing of targeting.

Another big consideration is that data is getting noisier. It's not just fairly uniform data such as a stream of transactions at Walmart or a series of demographic data that is creating this cacophony. Now there's audio data, video data, text, structured data, unstructured data. It is also the ad impressions accompanying your daughter's blogging by using social media. In this ceaseless exploding of information particles it's getting harder to extract the useful signal from the noise.

The goal is to get to a fine level of control. "You need to know why you're doing something before you even get to the question of what you should pay for it," says Joe Zawadzki. Once you ask why you're buying this data rather than that, it raises a few more fundamental questions. How good is the evidence that the data really works? How well is your online advertising achieving your ultimate marketing objectives? Focusing on clicks provides a reassuring sense that your direct-response advertising is producing *an effect*. That must be good, right?

Some in advertising see this presumption as an extremely shortsighted view that ignores the needs of brands. John Donahue, for example, CEO at an ad agency called White Lightning + Judge's Son, thinks we've created problems for ourselves in digital advertising.

Regarding the emphasis on clicks, Donahue says:

> By confusing impressions with [users'] responses to them [clicks], we've confused what our job is. Direct response is clutter that is driving us away from the fundamental goal of advertising: to excite

consumers about the core value proposition of the brand. We've confused a click with a user having actually established a relationship with a brand. In the competitive ad technology environment, there is too much temptation to take credit for creating a relationship [i.e., with a brand] that doesn't really exist. Technologies are [for] scaling, segmenting, or driving clicks, but they are not creating the awareness that marketers are hoping to achieve. [We're] chasing the wrong...thing.

Certainly, clicks are ambiguous. A click could be made by a user who intends to do what the advertiser is hoping to persuade him to do. At another time, it could be merely "snacking"—when we anxiously click to escape from work or distract ourselves. (See "Metrics That Matter," page 129.)

Data-Enabled Branding

Marketers often talk about "the funnel" as an illustration of the cycle of consideration that potential customers go through leading toward a purchase (at the bottom of the funnel). Branding—gaining awareness, consideration, favor, preference, recollection, and loyalty—is customarily shown at the top, the wide-open mouth of the funnel. It's the mental getting-to-know-you and realizing the advantages of the branded product or service that is presumed always to precede more active, direct responses by online users.

One novel use of data for branding is to conduct an experiment for a branding initiative that is like a double-blind clinical trial in new drug research. At the outset, a marketer selects a population substantial enough to be statistically significant and then shows an ad to 95 percent of them (the exposed group). The 5 percent who are not served the ad function as, in effect, the control group (the unexposed subgroup). Perhaps they are shown nothing. Or perhaps they are shown the equivalent of a placebo: a public service announcement.

Afterward, the marketer sends both groups what one ad tech CEO calls an "ADHD survey." It asks users one question about the branded product. The awareness shown by the unexposed group serves as the baseline and represents the general public's awareness. The amount by which favorability ticks up in the exposed group, as compared to the control group, is the effect showing the initial ad to 95 percent of the group had on branding.

An example of how this kind of data-enabled branding was used and paid off occurred in a campaign that Ford Motor Company ran in November 2010 for its new flagship 2011 line of top-selling F-Series trucks. The goal of the campaign was to make Internet users aware that the trucks had a new, higher-performance engine with best-in-class fuel economy.

This campaign had nothing to do with prompting a purchase in the near future. At any time, there are few in-market new car or truck buyers, so this was not direct-response advertising and click counting. Rather, Ford's goal was to optimize attitudes (change them to "I think this truck would be great to drive") rather than to elicit behaviors (such as ordering a brochure or locating a dealer). Moreover, Ford's agency, Team Detroit, a group of Ford specialists from several advertising and marketing agencies that are owned by WPP, knew that only three out of ten thousand users click on an ad. What, it wondered, could it do advantageously with the other 99.97 percent who saw the ad online? They also wondered how those 99.97 percent of users should be comprised and bought and for how much money.

In the old days, Ford's agency would have focused on whether the user went to Ford's site and asked for a brochure. This was a marketer-centric approach, not a customer-centric approach. In this case, Team Detroit didn't care if the traffic it was driving steered to Ford's site or to any site. It ran several different banners citing the new and improved features of the engine.

"In a campaign like this, it's less about where the ad is shown," says John Gray, a senior vice president at Team Detroit. "It's not crucial which site. Which audience segment sees the ad is more influential."

Working with DataXu, Team Detroit threw its net widely. It generated numerous segments: age and gender demographic segments, geographic segments, and sports enthusiast segments, among others. DataXu bought impressions on a lot of premium-content sites. It bought a select blend of exchange-traded media and comScore 250 sites.

Getting a huge initial sample (ultimately amounting to 28.8 million consumers) was crucial, because later on the agency planned to run a second ad with a one-question survey, and you have to start by exposing multitudes to the ad to get enough survey respondents to be statistically significant. Next, the agency chose a control group, who were not shown the ad extolling the new engine.

Throughout the campaign, DataXu and Team Detroit were comparing the change in awareness of the merits of the truck's new engine with the awareness of those merits shown by the control group. It correlated, on the fly, improvements in awareness and favorability with a number of factors: the ad's creativity, audience demographics, page content, day of the week, time of day, and geography, among others.

As the results were coming in, DataXu, in real time, targeted more members of the segments that showed the greatest gains in awareness or favorability (in ad jargon, this is called *brand lift*). At the same time, it assessed how much it had to pay to achieve the biggest differential lift (compared to the control group).

This guided the spending. Team Detroit put a steadily increasing share of dollars into buying impressions for segments where it was getting the most lift per dollar spent.

Of course, there were limits to allowing the numbers to drive this approach. For example, DataXu might have gotten the most lift for the least money from a segment that turned out to be truck-obsessed twelve-year-old boys. An algorithm might have shifted every cent in order to buy impressions targeting that segment. Although the agency didn't immediately have to sell a truck, it wasn't going to spend money paying for kids who didn't have driver's licenses. It wanted to move the brand-equity needle, but it didn't want to move the needle that badly.

Lift is great, but not all lift is created equal.

The key for Ford was using machine learning and data to drive marketing efficiencies. Without that real-time guidance to make the campaign continuously adaptive, the agency could not have hoped to make the most of its media investment. Before the advent of such ad technology online, making those changes in the campaign would have been too slow and cumbersome. Because learning what was working was happening constantly, and was incorporated on the fly into decisions for the rest of the campaign, the campaign got smarter the longer it ran.

In the end, the effect for branding was pronounced. DataXu's targeting achieved 9.4 percent greater favorability and a 5.8 percent improvement in awareness. It reached 28.8 million consumers showing an average of just 3.1 ads for each unique consumer.

"With this nearly real-time decisioning, we're learning whom to target and how much to pay for them," says John Gray of Team Detroit. "This is branding in the sense of creating new awareness by means of a highly optimized media investment."

Since then, Team Detroit has used this approach on all of its campaigns online. "This is like a table filled with little Petri dishes," says Gray, "experiments going on all the time. There's this continuous-improvement mindset that I really try to push in our team. We're constantly testing and learning, and changing and testing and learning. I find a lot of that in the digital subculture."

Data-Enabled Selling

In other chapters, I've mentioned data-enabled moves such as site retargeting or search retargeting that produce substantial improvements in user engagement. Much of that advertising would still fall under the heading of direct response rather than branding. But there are other, novel ways that branding is enhanced by the adroit use of data, even much later in the cycle or deeper down in the funnel.

One technology that has been experimented with employs the virtual shopping carts used at online retailers. Around 70 percent of shopping carts that contain merchandise are abandoned, no matter how great the brand affinity. The top two reasons for abandonment are price and time. As I said about online users in the Introduction: They can leave the web page where your ad appears with unprecedented ease and ... verging-on-anarchic nonallegiance.

Technology probably isn't going to help much if a user is really appalled by the price. But many users leave their loaded carts because other, higher-priority activities intrude, and the moment is lost.

The identifying data that advertisers use in targeting someone for an ad allows them to find that person elsewhere online and, like a little traveling salesperson perched on the user's cyber doorstep, offer the shopping cart still containing the merchandise the user had selected.

There are risks in this "did you forget something?" way of retargeting. Instead of viewing the cart as a helpful little droid like Wall-E, users might regard the shopping cart as, in effect, a bounty hunter stalking them as they surf the Web. There is a big risk that this new, data-enabled way of reconnecting with users could be seen as pushy, irritating, and creepy. (If the IRS collected taxes this way, it would no doubt create an uproar.)

On the other hand, there is no denying the convenience. If users really wanted to make a purchase, if their interrupted shopping was not just cyber tire kicking, they don't have to waste time going through the selection process again. The cart becomes, in effect, a camel in a caravan following them wherever they wander online. The shoppers can finish their purchases right in the display ad that presents the cart. They don't have to leave the site they are viewing. They don't have to click their way back to the retailer's site and hope their shopping cart is waiting for them.

In addition, if the users had some affinity for the brand and/or a strong desire for the merchandise, the convenience offered by this shopping cart tagging along after them could strengthen their affinity for the brand and make that relationship tighter.

Smart data–enabled targeting and selling sometimes involve knowing when to *stop* targeting. "The problem we run into is not that a user is being targeted," says Mike Baker, CEO of DataXu, "but that the targeting is not smart enough. It's too stale; it's not appreciating the time dimension. As an industry we're getting smart, but we're not yet smart enough."

Another, lesser-known use of data that affects brand affinity is using data to assess users' likely responsiveness in real time. For sales of most products there is a "decay curve" (see Figure 10–1). The vertical axis represents a user's likelihood of buying the product beginning with his or her initial exposure to an ad. The horizontal axis shows the decline in likelihood to buy over time. As this graph illustrates, the likelihood of buying typically declines sharply and quickly and then, as time passes, approaches zero by smaller and smaller steps.

Let's suppose a user had been browsing for casual slacks at the Nordstrom website. Let's also suppose that Nordstrom doesn't have multitudes of little cyber shopping carts to deploy to track the user all over the Internet and noodge him. In some cases, the decay curves for a given brand and a particular product can be very steep. The user's interest in such a product can decline to almost zero within as little as a minute.

The better informed the data and the more quickly it can be assessed, the more sensibly an advertiser can (1) make a quick effort to sell the slacks, (2) reduce what it would bid for a later exposure to that user, and then (3) pull the plug on advertising to that user.

For example, the analytics technology at DataXu continuously calculates decay curves for products for which it is running ad campaigns. It reduces what it will bid for impressions based on those results. It stops targeting a given user after a day, assuming that he has either bought the pants or lost interest in them. Either way, the user no longer warrants the investment in impressions, at any price.

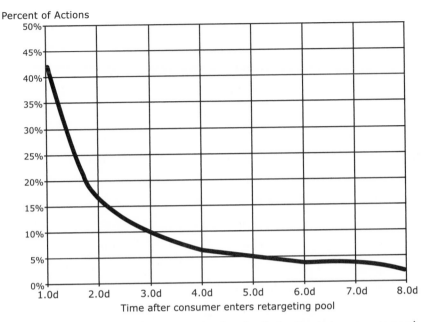

FIGURE 10-1   *This is a decay curve showing the diminution in target customers' purchasing as the time since they saw an ad increases. One day after being shown ads as part of a retargeting campaign, around 43 percent of users bought the merchandise. By day 8 after the retargeting, almost no customers made a purchase. A decay curve can also be seen as showing the rate of the extinction of the interest aroused by a retargeting ad campaign.   (Source: DataXu)*

Metrics That Matter

Data is not just for targeting. It's also a way to keep score. How well data is used, whether for direct-response advertising or for branding, depends a lot—not entirely, but a lot—on what advertisers choose to measure. Although it seems sort of cart-before-the-horse counterintuitive, the choice of metrics affects performance because it determines how and what we choose to count as results. Deciding *what* to count affects the decision about what *counts* as performance. And vice versa. You choose to count something because you've decided what satisfactory performance means.

You don't change a paradigm by changing one side of the equation. When you change a paradigm, you choose an entirely new equation.

This issue takes on added importance with branding because it's hard to correlate improvements in awareness with eventual sales. We all know there is a connection, but it's sketchy. According to Paul Verna, senior analyst at eMarketer, "Branding campaigns . . . are as difficult to measure in the digital domain as they are in traditional media."[2]

That's why measuring click-through rates has had such a big influence on online advertising. At least with click-through rates you can point to users taking an action when prompted by an ad they've seen online. The question is: How much should marketers rely on that sort of data?

A growing number of ad tech entrepreneurs, publishers, and commentators have expressed increasing concern about the predominance of and, perhaps, overreliance on click-through rates. While nobody expects clicks to be completely knocked off their pedestal as a measure of advertising effectiveness, some advocates have fired up their chain saws and are cutting that pedestal down a notch.

There are a number of reasons for the concern about clicks. As we saw earlier, some clicking is fairly meaningless ("snacking") behavior. Only around three out of ten thousand users who see an ad click on it. Looking at it through the other end of the telescope, "99.97 percent of the time ad impressions do not result in a click."[3] That's pretty weak evidence of effectiveness. Even when users *are* motivated by intent, clicks don't correlate very strongly to offline sales, and around 92 percent of sales are still offline.

But that low correlation is not surprising. Around three hundred million new websites were created worldwide in 2011, bringing the total number of websites on the Internet to perhaps over five hundred million. What graphic designer could depict that worldwide site map? The effect of all those outposts on the Internet is an experience of clutter, both among and within websites. Each of us is exposed to hundreds of ads each day, online and offline.

Even if those ads do blink for a moment on our mental radar screen, how much attention are we paying to them? Most people say that they don't click on ads. Although that's clearly untrue, it's hard to determine how much impact the ads are having.

Another problem is the fragmented way the Internet content and ads are presented. Every web page contains two or more ads. Every time you click, you are at a new page with new content and new ads. Because, online, we don't tend to be immersed as passively in the editorial or ad content as we are when we are watching the dramatic content of TV, the viewing experience is more scattered, distracting, and refractory to concentration.

Says Jonah Goodhart, founder of Moat, an analytics company for online display ads:

> Unlike when we're watching TV where the viewing experience is relatively consistent, the viewing experience of ads online is completely inconsistent. It depends on what site you're on, how big the ad is, where it was on the page, whether you scrolled down enough to see the entire ad, whether it had motion or sound that caught your attention, etc. Not to mention the fact that when we're online we're usually not sitting passively watching something, rather we're actively consuming. We're navigating. We're researching. We're messaging with friends. We're sharing photos. We're reading news or perhaps even doing work. What we're doing has a huge impact on whether or not we're likely to notice an ad.[4]

Consuming content in such circumstances, both editorial and advertising, can seem like trying to get a drink of water from a fire hose. New ad tech firms such as Moat are developing new metrics that provide more insight into what affects users' attitudes and actions, in the hopes that, guided by such metrics, the online user experience will be more congenial and the ads more effective.

CHAPTER 11

Data Collection and Its Effect on Privacy

I n 1787, British philosopher and social reformer Jeremy Bentham traveled to Krichev in White Russia and, with his brother Samuel, developed a radically new idea for a prison, which he called the "Panopticon."[1] What made his concept so different was that the inmates could be watched at all times, and they knew it. Cruel and unusual? Bentham called it "a new mode of obtaining power of mind over mind."[2] Whether this new model prison would have reformed or punished better than others that then existed was never determined. It was not built. What remains significant about the Panopticon is that, to a late-eighteenth-century social reformer such as Bentham, the most effective punishment imaginable was to eliminate every last scrap of privacy a person had.

How times have changed. A new social video network and live chat service called Airtime.com was launched June 5, 2012. The network was cofounded by Sean Parker, a former president of Facebook and a cofounder of Napster, the music-file-sharing service. For now, Airtime enrolls only Facebook users. Click a button and every tidbit of your Facebook profile is automatically transferred to your Airtime account. That includes your name, picture, gender, education, interests, location, religion, political views, and work history, among a multitude of other data. By consenting to Airtime's terms, you have permitted its app to post *on your behalf* (without requiring any permission in the event) information about any videos you watched, any videos you added, and more. Who can see those video posts? The terms state: "This [app] does not control who can see your activity within the app itself and when you are tagged in the app...."

The locution "does not control" makes it sound as if the sharing is done indiscriminately, unselectively. That's not quite accurate. The algorithm tries to interest-match you and any strangers (i.e., those who are not your Facebook friends) and then introduces you to them. Once you've invoked that fateful initial opt-in, an indiscriminate sharing happens automatically. It's all done by algorithm, and while your Airtime match may share some of your interests, who knows what or how many differences you and your match may have? It's an algorithmically setup blind date, with all the potential pitfalls blind dates are known for.

Moreover, your consent allows Airtime to monitor the video chats you have with strangers by taking (presumably occasional and random) screenshots of the chat, which Airtime indicates is for your protection, of course.

Granted, Airtime is voluntary. Unlike the Panopticon, you are not convicted of a crime and sentenced to Airtime. You must opt in. But, from the standpoint of exposure to surveillance at times not of your choosing and conducted by technology, there seems to be plenty of similarity between Airtime and the Panopticon.

A growing multitude of privacy advocates, here and abroad, are bemoaning the extent to which our privacy has been subverted by such online services as well as by the tracking being done by advertisers. The commercial sharing of data about you that is used for behavioral targeting for advertising purposes is being done without your permission. Your privacy is being encroached upon continually without your awareness. This has spawned outcries and protests, a trickle of class action lawsuits from plaintiffs who feel their privacy has been infringed upon, and proposals for stricter regulation by the U.S. government.

A Federal Trade Commission preliminary staff report states:

> In today's digital economy, consumer information is more important than ever.... Although many ... companies manage consumer information responsibly, some appear to treat it in an irresponsible or even reckless manner.... [M]any companies—both online and offline—do not adequately address consumer privacy interests. Industry must do better. For every business, privacy should be a basic consideration—similar to keeping track of costs and revenues, or strategic planning.
>
> The application of [the] concept [of privacy] in modern times is by no means straightforward. Consumers live in a world where information about their purchasing behavior, online browsing habits, and other online and offline activity is collected, analyzed, combined, used, and shared, often instantaneously and invisibly.[3]

The European Union promulgated strict regulations about online tracking, established criminal penalties for breaches of privacy, and required opt-in protocols.

To some extent, the vehemence of this reaction is an understandable response to the different pace of the development of technology and the social norms about it. Technology always moves faster than the development of ways to manage it. We can do way more, way faster with technology, and in developing technology, than we can create laws or regulations to harness it.

"The development of sophistication in managing the technology from a governance, compliance, and consumer-protection perspective ... that is not a fast process," says J. Trevor Hughes, an attorney and CEO of the International Association of Privacy Professionals. "Yet the development of technology is a fast process. It obeys Moore's law."

But the concerns of privacy advocates are much more than anxiety about the rush of technology. The tidal wave set off by the Internet and our networked digital devices has leveled the dikes around our personal privacy and carried away much of our *personally identifying information* (PII). This has happened explosively and at such a speed that it defies transparency, let alone awareness. That gives many the feeling that something insidious is going on that is outracing our ability to comprehend and control it. How real a threat are online technologies to our privacy?

The Trouble with Cookies

A lot of people have heard about cookies being planted in their computers without their awareness or consent, so let's begin with them. In the fourth quarter of 2013, an estimated 138 billion cookies were put on U.S. computers every day.[4] Earlier, I discussed the browser cookies that most people are suspicious about, which typically contain no PII. They are just short strings of code, which, as I said earlier, is like wearing a name tag without your name on it. But a publishing company, advertiser, or their affiliates can tell that they placed a cookie on your computer. This sort of cookie, even without PII, helps advertisers and ad technology companies connect you and your networked device to other profiles of you being kept and continually updated at online exchanges, DSPs, SSPs, advertisers, and data providers.

Users who don't want to be tracked can fairly easily erase such cookies.[5] But, almost as soon as you turn around, you'll find that new tracking cookies have been placed on your computer. Who has the time, fastidiousness, or diligence to stay on top of this, to delete cookies repeatedly and perpetually? No one who has a life.

As the profiles about you, your browsing, and your shopping habits become more detailed, it is self-deluding to think that you're not being identified. At some point there is so much information about you being logged and stored in so many places that any marketer, hacker, political operative, or government agency that wanted to could learn as much about you (even your name and address) as they could if they had your social security number or credit card information. To depend for one's privacy on the fact that the cookie itself does not have your name or can be erased is a flimsy recourse and very fragile assurance. If they can find you wherever you are and make you encounter what they want you to encounter, how much privacy do you really have? Every move you make is like going through a scanner at the security checkpoint at the airport.

In part, this self-delusion and denial about the loss of our privacy persists because of an unwarranted trust that if our personally identifying information is kept confidential then our privacy is ensured. Of course, such PII—your social security number, bank account numbers, credit card numbers, and passwords—are the crown jewels of your privacy. And just as the crown jewels are guarded in the Tower of London, your PII is worth protecting carefully.

The problem is, as technology advances rapidly and data rustlers capture more specific information about you, including your zip code, gender, and household income, the various combinations of this extant, easily obtainable data—to distinguish it from PII, let's use the nomenclature of British entrepreneur John Taysom and call it *identifiably personal information* (IPI)—can be used to identify you just as uniquely and effectively as your PII can. If an advertiser can know accurately how much you're paid at work, your credit score, your method of birth control, your zip code, your gender, your medical records,[6] and whether you've ever been arrested or are pregnant,[7] then they've reached a point at which they can identify you with pinpoint accuracy, even if they don't know your name or social security number. What does your privacy amount to at that point?

Let's assume, however, that, because of your unceasing vigilance, you constantly erase browser cookies from your computer. Furthermore, let's assume you're such a computer whiz that you've even created a program that automatically removes browser cookies the minute they are put in your computer. (You smugly consider calling the program "Cookie Crumbler" or "Cookie Monster," and wonder if you can sell the app at the App

Store and make a bundle. *Who knew you were such an entrepreneur?* But then, how are you going to target potential customers?) Would that be enough to safeguard your privacy? No.

That's because there are other, more refractory privacy–infringing cookies. Browser cookies are only the most common, least–threatening sorts to compromise our privacy. For example, there are other cookies, called *super cookies, flash cookies,* or *local shared objects* (LSOs) that are so persistent they are virtually inerasable. Browser cookies are to flash cookies as a brief visit from an insurance salesperson is to a seemingly endless visit to your dentist.

How hard is it to get rid of flash cookies? You practically need a degree in computer science from MIT. Such cookies can and sometimes do serve legitimate functions, such as enabling your computer to mute or unmute the sound track of videos. So it's good that they are squatters you can't evict from your computer. Their presence ensures that they can serve such functions whenever it's necessary. That's the beneficial rationale for their persistence. But there is nothing to stop crafty hackers or marketers from using flash cookies for reasons that are illegitimate or manipulative. In those cases, their resistance to being erased borders on being wicked.

Let's say, though, that your cookie–deleting program can rid your computer even of flash cookies. (Maybe you should call your app "Cookie Genocide.") Unfortunately, your privacy is still not secure.

There is certain information that your computer has about itself that is called the *user agent string.* All our computers have certain hardware and software, as well as a very specific and individuating history of how they have been modified and updated, including what plug–ins you've installed, what browsers you're running, and what sort of coding the computer can interpret. The user agent string expresses in one sequence of digital code that very specific roster of your computer's componentry, software, and other functional attributes.

The user agent string can function like a Trojan horse. It can be used to track you. It works like this. In combination with your computer's IP address (which is not exactly or enduringly unique; nevertheless, it narrows things down to your device and to you, or pretty close to you), the user agent string can serve as your device's signature.

Furthermore, combining flash cookies with the user agent string is also undeletable. Other similar, cookie-less ways of tracking you are device fingerprinting, machine fingerprinting, or browser fingerprinting. All are variants on the user agent string. None of these is foolproof, thankfully, but all can ominously home in on you. So, even if you could completely eradicate cookies, that will not protect you from being tracked.

Unfortunately, there are plenty of other threats. There are programs called *spyware* that beguile you to install insidiously troublesome software onto your computer. Buried in the small print of the multipage license agreement you sign is a clause that grants (that is, by agreeing, you are granting) the spyware vendor permission to install its toolbar in your computer. That enables the vendor to deluge you with pop-up ads that are nearly impossible to stop or delete. Spyware vendors are getting paid to do that on behalf of advertisers. They are like intrusive barkers who figuratively grab you by the collar and shout in your face. Suddenly and unintentionally, you've become the moving-target duck in an advertising shooting gallery. Spyware manipulates your computer to make the spyware operator a profit and make you an unwitting stooge in that process.

Reidentification

Earlier, we drew a distinction between personally identifying information (PII) and identifiably personal information (IPI). The PII is fixed and thought to be more valuable. These are the items that, if revealed, identify you uniquely and most irremediably. For this reason, PII usually is guarded most carefully.

By contrast, IPI is a blizzard of information, much of it seemingly random and innocuous. We tend to treat it as being of low value (that is, for privacy preservation). Much of this data is in the public domain.

As we've seen, PII isn't the only way your privacy can be infringed upon or invaded. Put enough IPI together and it will "out" you just as accurately. Almost any information can be identifying when combined with additional pertinent and useful bits that have your figurative fingerprints on them. From the standpoint of privacy preservation, the distinction between PII and IPI pretty much breaks down. IPI can become uniquely identifying nowadays, as more about you is disclosed and searchable and as technology (algorithms, search capabilities, storage in databases, for example) advances. What couldn't identify you yesterday can identify you today, or soon will.

This has created the new science of reidentification. This science enables your privacy to be breached; cookies, real-time tracking, or user agent strings are not necessary. Reidentification science identifies you deductively, using, in some cases, the most incredibly mundane IPI that is available everywhere—and it doesn't take a Sherlock Holmes to do it. Advances in reidentification enable the widespread identification of individuals even without the disclosure of their PII. Unfortunately, we've all left way too many telltale clues lying around.

For example, during the mid-1990s the Group Insurance Commission (GIC), which purchased health insurance for state employees in Massachusetts, released a database of medical records of state employees, including every hospital visit. The data supposedly had been "anonymized." It had been scrubbed clean of PII. At the time the data was released, Governor William Weld assured the public that the database disclosure protected patient privacy because all identifiers had been deleted.

A graduate student named Latanya Sweeney decided to see if she could identify state employees and match them with their medical records using the database. She picked Governor Weld as her first target.

Knowing that he lived in Cambridge, with a population of 54,000 in seven zip codes, Sweeney bought a database containing the city voter rolls for $20. This provided her with the name, address, zip code, birth date, and gender of everyone who voted in the city. Using this data, along with the

Group Insurance Commission records, she easily identified Governor Weld: Only six people on the rolls shared his birth date, only three of whom were men, and only Weld lived in the right zip code. So Sweeney sent the governor's health records, including diagnoses and prescriptions, to his office, letting him know that his assurances about privacy didn't hold up.[8]

In 2000, Sweeney, then a professor at Carnegie Mellon University, using publicly available data from the 1990 census, demonstrated that 87 percent of Americans could be uniquely identified using only three items of information about them: zip code, date of birth, and gender.[9] All of this data is in databases that are widely available. The identifications made by Sweeney used data—such as zip code, date of birth, and gender—that most of us would think of as at least pertinent to our identity, if not personally identifying information.

Still other studies have shown that such pertinent-to-identity data isn't even necessary. We can be identified by far more humdrum, not-very-personal-seeming data. For example, in October 2006, Netflix released a database of a hundred million records disclosing how nearly a half million of its customers rated movies from December 1999 to December 2005. In each instance, Netflix cited the name of the movie, the rating (from one to five stars), and when the film was rated. Before releasing the database, Netflix removed all PII (but it gave each customer a unique index number). After the release of the database, a study by researchers at the University of Texas showed that, by using their ratings of just three movies, it was possible to identify accurately more than 80 percent of Netflix customers.[10] The researchers, Arvind Narayanan and Vitaly Shmatikov, were using movie ratings—hardly what would be considered PII. They showed, moreover, that, if they knew when a customer rated six movies (with a two-week margin of error), no matter which movies, they could identify the person correctly 99 percent of the time. Knowing when only two movies were rated enabled a correct identification more than two-thirds (68 percent) of the time.[11]

What to make of such capabilities of reidentification technology? For starters, it should disabuse us of our assumption that, as long as we guard a few nuggets of high-value identifiers (our PII), we've kept our privacy intact. Clearly, that's no longer true. As Professor Paul Ohm, of the University of Colorado Law School, writes:

> Re-identification science disrupts the privacy policy landscape by undermining the faith we have placed in anonymization. This is no small faith, for technologists rely on it to justify sharing data indiscriminately and storing data perpetually, while promising users (and the world) that they are protecting privacy. Advances in re-identification expose these promises as too often illusory.[12]

As these various, appallingly on-target IDs in reidentification science show, faith in anonymization is far worse than naïve credulity. It is, as Bentham might have said, "nonsense upon stilts."

These few examples of privacy-compromising technologies, from cookies to something as innocuous and seemingly ephemeral as movie ratings, are by no means exhaustive or confined to online advertising. I could cite plenty of others. Suffice it to say that the means exist to track and identify you. Technology enables sleazy geeks to invade your privacy, and there is probably not much you can do about it. If anybody wants to, they can get you.

That doesn't mean that your privacy necessarily has been or will be confiscated. But, whatever your privacy once was, it's now like a single tissue buried in a titanic box of tissues. That's how thin your anonymity is. You may be secure for a while. But when the world wants the tissue that corresponds to you, it won't take much concerted effort to get it and later dispose of it as the world decides.

Most data privacy laws try to foil invasions of privacy by restricting access to PII. We've seen the limited efficacy of that deterrent. The measures taken to make privacy laws and regulation more protective will, writes

Nate Anderson, "increase privacy or reduce the utility of data, but there will be no way to guarantee maximal usefulness and maximal privacy at the same time."[13]

In Europe, the European Union Data Protection Directive (officially Directive 95/46/EC on the protection of individuals with regard to the processing of personal data and on the free movement of such data) requires that Internet service providers (ISPs) and publishers offer prospective users the option to opt in or not, and clearly stipulate what users must consent to if they opt in. The regulations promulgated pursuant to the directive also provide criminal penalties for obtaining and using data not authorized by users beforehand.

Even if privacy infringement was criminalized, as in Europe, and could be caught before the perpetrators got your private information, and even if people are offered the option of more diligently protecting themselves, probably it won't happen. As Shakespeare wrote in *Julius Caesar*, "... the fault ... is not in our stars, but in ourselves." Why?

The Internet has encouraged and enabled a surrender of privacy on a scale that hasn't been exhibited by any other medium. Technology aside, there is a vast variety of ways you voluntarily disclose data, not all of them online. Let's tick off some of the ways you spew identifiably personal information:

→ When you register at a website in order to compete in a sweepstakes

→ When you seek tech support for a product

→ When you comment on an article you read online

→ When you register merchandise you've just purchased

→ When you subscribe to an online version of a publication

→ When you make a purchase at a retail store or online and use a loyalty card or loyalty card information

→ When you make a credit card transaction at a gas station

→ When you do opt-in to data sharing when enrolling in or using a social app or website such as Facebook or Twitter

→ When you are tracked by the use of geolocation data on your cell phone or other GPS-enabled device

→ When you do a Google search

These are just a few examples illustrating how you strew IPI in the wake you create by your various activities using digital media. We all do this. Such a torrent of what is, basically, self-expression, worldwide, dwarfs into insignificance the effects of deterrence, containment, or the vigilance that very few of us can muster. When thousands of people thousands of times a day rush to tell their five hundred *closest* (?) friends about the sneakers they just bought, how could any countermeasures combined cope with this torrential outpouring of the multitudinous minutiae of unprotected us?

To a great extent, this subversion of our privacy is, in effect, a defect of the Internet's virtues. We give up so much of our privacy because the Internet offers so many benefits that we want and for which we have grown dependent on it. No other medium is so interactive and enables us to find so much for ourselves. No TV programmer, however obsessed with ratings and trying to appeal to viewers, has ever assessed the actual attitudes of the audience with the precision that is revealed by people through their voluntary browsing behavior.

Our privacy repeatedly gets surrendered in the act of using the Internet to meet needs that, in the moment, are a higher priority than our desire for privacy. Kevin O'Connor, the cofounder and former CEO of Double-Click, recalls a study reporting that people would give their social security number in return for free shipping. "That means that their social security number is worth around six dollars [that is, to them]," says O'Connor.

We repeatedly sacrifice privacy for practical advantage. Yet, it's in the nature of privacy that the loss of it is something we experience and may regret only later, after the fact. In the meantime, we've gotten something we wanted more urgently. That's not necessarily a bad thing, is it? No, it's not—necessarily. It depends how good the trade-offs are. But we should be mindful of the trade-offs we're making as we make them, not after, when it's too late to rectify them. Six dollars?

Suppose we lived in a democracy that did not use secret ballots. Suppose it was not a republic, as ours is, in which we elected representatives to serve in a legislature to vote on our behalf on proposed laws. Instead, voters were polled on political issues all the time, perhaps every day, perhaps more often. Every day (or more) there would be a plebiscite, a vote of all citizens. This would be a pure and very public democracy. Such a system would also be the political equivalent of death by a thousand paper cuts. Our voting record would be compiled, and everyone could know how everyone, especially their neighbors, voted on every issue. Every person would be his or her own congressperson, always on call. What would you think of that sort of system?

With the Internet and online tracking, we're participating in the commercial analog of such a system, only the voting we're doing is the allocation of our attention. In this case, others are compiling our browsing behavior and other data about us. Moreover, we're voting more often than if we were voting on only political issues, where we would be voting only on referenda and proposed legislation. But with the Internet, we are accessing and voting by our browsing behavior and the attention we bestow on so many more issues than those that are political. Where to vacation? What to buy? The research we conduct for ourselves. The medicines we consider taking. The music we download. The videos we watch. All our social interactions on Facebook and other social media.

We think we're voting in secret. We're not. In the plebiscite example, our neighbors could know how we voted; on the Internet, others do know exactly how we're behaving. That's the part that's secret. We aren't very aware of it. Are you beginning to care more about giving out your data without thinking much about that? Given the enormous volume of interactions that we have and wish to have, there is no way we could be vigilant enough to withhold our consent to opt in on each occasion. We would very quickly become fatigued by the vigilance required to do so. In view of the avalanche of interaction worldwide at all times and the benefits that we get from it right now, who could govern the data transfers in a way that preserved our privacy as we would like, even if we were well informed about what we're giving up and what others were doing with our data?

Could the Monetized Retaliate?

Suppose we couldn't govern the data transfers to preserve our privacy. Perhaps we could monetize it in a way that was at least better for us. What if people, as they became better informed, became more hard-nosed about the trade-offs in which they were participating unthinkingly. Trade-offs go smoothly until someone suggests a quid pro quo that is going to cost some serious money. Our privacy is already being monetized. It's just being monetized in a way that doesn't sufficiently reward us. The Internet is a dollar store of our surrendered privacy. What if people in large numbers demanded much better compensation in exchange for their privacy?

People assume they are *adequately* compensated for their attention and the surrender of their data. The compensation has been considered adequate because people have been unaware of the extent and the low value they've tacitly granted for their data. What happens if people demand compensation for the use of their data, whether personally identifying or not? Imagine this scenario: Internet users en masse demand of publishers, marketers, and advertising agencies, "You've just monetized my behavior. Pay me."

Sure, it sounds far-fetched. Who would care if a few extremists advocated it? But what if this was the cause of action in a class action suit with multimillions of plaintiffs? Even before the suit came before a judge, because there were so many plaintiffs, it would be unlikely or maybe impossible to settle with some but not others or to tell them, "Okay, we won't use your data or target you." Does that sound like a persuasive settlement approach? Not if the class of plaintiffs grew larger, along with the payoff they'd expect. Suddenly something looks even worse than more government regulation.

That's an extreme worst case, of course, and probably unlikely. (We'll talk about legal remedies in the next section.) But what if those forming the biggest bulge under the bell curve become increasingly pragmatic—and politically active—about being compensated for their privacy? "What do I get, if you have access to, manipulate, or make money from my data?" they may ask. Likely or not, it's not that difficult to envision. If the number of people involved in the movement was large enough, the government might actually enact laws requiring payment when people were made to view intrusive advertising or give up their privacy when visiting a site.

Legal Remedies

As the public has become more conscious of how its privacy has been compromised, there has been a series of class action lawsuits complaining about invasions of privacy. Such legal recourses have not worked out well. In many cases, especially in jurisdictions in the vicinity of Silicon Valley, the suits have been thrown out of court before they were even argued, because the plaintiffs could not establish that they had really been injured, at least, not in a way that made sense to the judge.

In litigation there is a concept called *standing*. You can't get the court to pay attention to you unless you have standing to sue. To have standing, you have to be able to show convincingly that you have suffered in some way and that the harm is attributable to the defendant (the person or firm being sued).

So what's the problem for privacy plaintiffs? Judges often preside over cases in which people can prove gigantic dollar losses because of fraud or had the wrong arm or leg cut off because of surgical error. Not surprisingly, judges used to hearing such convincing evidence of harm have not been very receptive to claims by plaintiffs that their privacy was infringed, which may have made them feel a bit creepy. Case dismissed.

"The complaints really boil down to a fear factor about what's new," says S. Ashlie Beringer, the deputy general counsel at Facebook. Before joining Facebook, Beringer defended high-tech firms such as Apple, Specific Media, and Yelp against class action privacy lawsuits and succeeded in getting several of the cases thrown out of court. "Standing is a huge, hot-button issue," she says. "To what extent do new tracking technologies and new advertising models actually result in legally sufficient harm?"

In 2012, however, a case called *First American Financial Corp. v. Edwards* reached the Supreme Court. Because the Court left the lower court's ruling intact, it may make judges in lower courts less inclined to dismiss privacy complaints.

The *First American Financial* case didn't even concern a privacy issue. It was about kickbacks and collusion in the real estate financial services business, but it did have bearing on the issue of standing. As the case worked its way through one court after another, the allegedly sleazy bank that was the defendant (First American Financial Corp.) started getting support from high-tech companies such as Facebook, LinkedIn, Yahoo!, and Zynga, as well as Experian and the Consumer Data Industry Association. Why the interest of such technology big guns?

A key claim in the suit filed by Edwards was that it was judicially sufficient to establish standing if it could be shown that there had been a violation of some protection or right explicitly granted by a law, whether or not any financial or other harm could be demonstrated. Just the fact that someone's rights granted by statute were violated was enough to provide standing. Of course, if this principle was countenanced by the courts, then any number of lawsuits over breaches of privacy could be filed without the likelihood of or being vulnerable to being thrown out of court before trial because of lack of standing.

When the case was argued in the Ninth Circuit Court of Appeals, in

San Francisco, the appeals court found[14] that "Congress has the power to create standing by defining legal rights and injuries."[15] This established that Edwards had standing to sue.

The case was appealed to the Supreme Court, which agreed, in 2011, to hear the case and did. However, on June 28, 2012, rather than rendering a decision, the Supreme Court reversed itself, saying it had been a mistake to accept the case in the first place. That left standing (no pun intended) the decision of the appeals court, which favored Edwards, the plaintiff. It also makes privacy lawsuits less likely to be summarily dismissed.

The outcome of the First American Financial case may be a turning point that is advantageous for plaintiffs in privacy suits. That will depend on how consistently the principle of standing is applied by lower court judges. Even if it is applied consistently, what it amounts to is that plaintiffs now can sue, knowing that, at a minimum, their cases will be heard. That's far from assuring them of a victory, however. For now, the question remains: How useful is a lawsuit as a recourse for redressing privacy-loss grievances?

In law there is an old adage: Your rights are a function of your remedies. If the law doesn't do much to make you whole from some loss, even if you are victorious in court, then how robust were your rights in the first place?

The twists and turns of the First American Financial case exemplify what happens in lots of lawsuits. Time is wasted. Expenses are huge. Results aren't known until the last minute, and the decision could go against you. Your cause of action could be entirely just, in your opinion, and your lawyer could mess up.

The vagaries of lawsuits aside, let's consider their efficacy. Let's say you're suing over a privacy issue. While your case is slowly grinding its way through courts, is your lost privacy being rehabbed or restored satisfactorily? That's probably more doubtful than the outcome of the case. There is a high risk that such legal recourses will be exercises in futility.

Furthermore, the minimal efficacy of lawsuits for reclaiming privacy cannot be blamed only on apathetic judges. What about the influence of *our* conduct as the guardians of our privacy? As Harvard Law School professor Noah Feldman writes:

> It seems that every time you ride the bus you hear one-half of the most intimate conversations imaginable—emanating from a total stranger with a phone to his ear. The justices [of the Supreme Court] cannot help but be affected by these trends [in technology use]. Privacy is defined constitutionally by "reasonable expectation" of what should be private.... The concept of privacy is inherently flexible, and the less we value it, the less our judicial institutions will protect it for us.[16]

Do-Not-Track Initiatives

Earlier, I ticked off a list of benefits that many of us get from using the Internet. The list could have been much longer. The Internet is an enormous public service that we get for free. We don't subscribe to the Internet. It isn't like a cable TV service. We don't pay for *most* of the useful content we get. We don't pay Google or other search engines for the searches they do for us. We don't pay travel sites for the information we use for planning and booking our trips. We all know we would hate to lose the convenience and gratification the Internet offers. The understood quid pro quo is that we must tolerate being bombarded by the advertising.

However, it's one thing to put up with a cockney-sounding gecko or a duck quacking in our faces, it's another to acquiesce to ad tech firms, data firms, advertisers, their agencies, and online ad exchanges amassing ever-more-detailed profiles of our behavior online or off. Companies should be free to engage in lawful commerce, but their right to conduct commerce surely isn't unlimited in its intrusiveness, is it?

That sentiment has given rise to a renewed impetus for Do-Not-Track (DNT) initiatives. Microsoft has announced that its newest version of Internet Explorer would have the DNT option as the preselected default. Users would have to go to some trouble to turn off DNT.

But a Do–Not–Track recourse raises other questions. How feasible would it be? Wouldn't a DNT program put several legitimate firms out of business? Should firms regulate themselves or be regulated by some outside or governmental authority? It's virtually certain that some firms will violate the regulations, however they are imposed. How could they be enforced? What sort of penalties should be levied on firms that don't comply?

Do–Not–Track programs sound good because they have a comforting-seeming similarity to the Do–Not–Call programs that have been used to reduce the number of telemarketing phone calls. But Do–Not–Track programs are not like Do–Not–Call programs in other respects.

There is only one way that telemarketers intrude on us: by telemarketing phone calls. But there are so many ways and instances in which we hand over data—on our own initiative—on the Internet. When we register at websites to participate in a sweepstakes or as new owners of a product, enroll for tech support or cloud storage services, or shop online, among a multitude of other interactions, we give up information about ourselves. We make such disclosures using a growing multitude of different devices—computers, smartphones, tablets, TV set–top boxes—or at point–of–sale terminals at retailers or online. But with this ceaseless iteration of occasions in which we give away identifiably personal information, for so many different reasons, it is increasingly doubtful that there will be a "magic privacy button."[17] Says Adam Lehman, COO and president at Lotame, a data management platform (DMP), "DNT tools will limit data activities in certain areas...but these tools are not equipped (and likely can't ever be constructed) to regulate the full range of data relationships between consumers and companies."[18]

As I said earlier, in the European Union users must be presented with the option and need to ponder whether to opt in before making use of content in the first instance at a publisher's site. But, as with many privacy disclosures, despite (or perhaps because of) the ominous and onerous small print that most folks do not read carefully, such opt-in requirements put everyone in the position of having to choose between the immediate gratification of a benefit and the later hypothetical-seeming and obscure loss of an abstract-seeming right. Few would eschew reading the *Financial Times* of London while they eat their breakfast each morning in return for giving to the *Financial Times* the right to slice and dice their data. As a practical matter, human nature makes it difficult to give up something we want now in exchange for some nebulous future protective benefit. It would take a truly obsessive lawyer type to give such opt-ins the careful consideration they deserve.

On May 1, 2014 President Obama's Council of Advisors on Science and Technology (PCAST) issued a report to the president that acknowledged the unfairness and failings of such "notice-and-consent" or "opt-in" procedures as a way of protecting our privacy. The Report to the President states:

> Notice and consent is, today, the most widely used strategy for protecting consumer privacy.... In some fantasy world, users actually read these notices, understand their legal implications...and only then click to indicate their consent. Reality is different.
>
> Notice and consent fundamentally places the burden of privacy protection on the individual—exactly the opposite of what is usually meant by a "right." Worse yet, if it is hidden in such a notice that the provider has the right to share personal data, the user normally does not get any notice from the next company, much less the opportunity to consent, even though use of the data may be different. Furthermore, if the provider changes its privacy notice for the worse, the user is typically not notified in a useful way.
>
> As a useful policy tool, notice and consent is...simply too complicated for the individual to make fine-grained choices for every new situation or app....
>
> One way to view the problem with notice and consent is that it creates a non level playing field in the implicit privacy negotiation

between provider and user. The provider offers a complex take it or leave it set of terms, backed by a lot of legal firepower, while the user, in practice, allocates only a few seconds of mental effort to evaluating the offer, since acceptance is needed to complete the transaction that was the user's purpose, and since the terms are typically difficult to comprehend quickly. This is a kind of market failure.[19]

The fault here is not in the technology. It is wonderfully prolific in providing solutions to our needs even as it occasionally is used for bad or, at least, objectionable purposes. But our technology exists within the larger realm of culture, and ours is a culture of surrender where privacy is concerned. Our cultural disposition is to disclose IPI, and that's what should be scrutinized at least as thoughtfully as the technological tools or the companies upon which we project the blame.

John Taysom's "Three Is a Crowd"

While most news stories about privacy have quoted concerned advocates deploring the loss of it, few have offered constructive, practical suggestions for fixing the problem, other than calling for operating constraints such as Do–Not–Track regulations.

Meanwhile, a British media executive and venture capitalist, John Taysom, has been developing a novel approach for shoring up our eroding personal privacy, an initiative that is both markedly different from other proposals and likely to be feasible without government oversight or the need for more onerous regulation. Taysom's privacy technology was granted a patent by the European Union, and recently he was notified by the U.S. Patent Office that it would be approving his patent application. Taysom has met with technology policymakers at both the White House and the U.S. Department of Commerce, who have been intrigued by the fact that his privacy program doesn't require government regulations. On July 16, 2012, the day Taysom was notified that his European patent application had been granted, he met at 10 Downing Street with one of British prime minister David Cameron's key advisers on technology and entrepreneurialism.

In 1995, Taysom, a former senior Reuters executive, negotiated the rules governing the placement of ads on Yahoo! web pages that contained Reuters' news. Later, as founder and CEO of the Greenhouse Fund, a Reuters-owned venture capital firm based in Silicon Valley, he became more familiar with the privacy implications of technology firms he considered investing in. Under Taysom's direction, the Greenhouse Fund was extremely successful.

Taysom's plan, called "Three Is a Crowd," is a way to reclaim and resecure our tenuously tethered identifiably personal information. In some ways, it resembles the Superfund-financed remediation of a toxic waste site.

When Taysom presented his proposed privacy program while participating in 2012 as a fellow in Harvard's Advanced Leadership Initiative (ALI), it impressed Dr. Jim Waldo, chief technology officer for Harvard University and a privacy authority of stature who teaches Harvard's multidisciplinary course on privacy.

Explaining why they asked Taysom to participate in ALI, Professor Rosabeth Moss Kanter, the head of ALI's admissions committee, said: "John Taysom is imaginative and often thinks in counter-intuitive ways. We chose [John] because of his ... eye for trends, success at forming technology ventures or facilitating their development, and superb skills as a networker who can connect people from disparate organizations."

Taysom's program has three main features. The first is a redundantly protected online repository of personal information. The second is a not-for-profit, nongovernmental institution that administers the program. This institution is in some ways similar to what in Britain are called Community Interest Companies, which are designed to benefit the community rather than private shareholders. It can also be likened to the Internet Corporation for Assigned Names and Numbers (ICANN), which administers naming on the Internet. An analog in the United States might be Underwriters Laboratories (UL), which is an independent, not-for-profit product safety testing and certification organization.

Third and crucially, the program shares information that would be useful to advertisers but does so only by concealing individuals in clusters of similar people. Before it disseminates information that could be attributed to a particular person, it combines such information into real-time assembled "crowds" of look-alikes that are sufficiently large and comprised so as to thwart anyone or any firm from using the information to discover the identity of the person it came from.

It's an exercise in algorithmic concealment that to a very high degree of probability prevents tracing back to the individual or the IP address of his or her device. You and your identity stay confidential because you merge undetectably into the crowd of people with whom you are similar in ways you're not concerned about revealing. You become like one nail in a bag of nails.

Taysom and his partner, Dr. David Cleevely, founding director of the Centre for Science and Policy, University of Cambridge, and one of Britain's ranking experts in mobile communications and security, have patented the approach and the algorithm that makes it work.

"The construction of the databases [entailed by Taysom's program] is straightforward and doable," says Harvard's Waldo. "The anonymizing of the data is new, but I think it's quite feasible. I don't see any particular technological difficulty that would make it impossible."

This approach, in effect, reclaims privacy for your information. But it also provides advertisers with the characteristics that make all members of the crowd worthwhile targets for ads. The marketer gets to present ads to a group of likely-to-be-responsive viewers but can never know the individual IP addresses or the identities of those to whom the ad has been presented.

"One of the keys to this approach is the recognition that, to advertisers, what makes an individual valuable are the attributes they share with others, rather than the traits they don't share with many that make them unique individuals and identifiable," says Taysom.

Because of this insight, Taysom's proposal is the first one that meets both a person's need for privacy and advertisers' need for audience targeting.

Taysom is not well known outside a small circle of people in the tech industry, Silicon Valley, and Harvard. But, with the patents granted and the recent meetings with both the United States and British government policymakers, his initiative is picking up steam.

There are a number of reasons why Taysom's proposed program is worth considering. He has framed the privacy issue differently from others. He is not just espousing one side of the regulation vs. no regulation dispute or the opt-in vs. opt-out conflict. His plan requires no expansion of government regulation. It requires no government oversight or growth in bureaucracy. He is willing to imagine institutions and solutions not yet created. He is commendably audacious, in the public interest. He views privacy in a more expansive way than most commentators. Finally, he alone has conceived of a recourse that promises to be beneficial for all parties, changing it from the current zero-sum game in which advertisers get to sell without hindrance and you become a set of eyeballs that are trackable and under their control.

"What John's program does is it allows the decisions on privacy to be made by the people themselves," says Waldo. "Until now decisions about people's privacy have been made by governments, by companies, or by the Mark Zuckerbergs. John's approach lets people decide for themselves how much of their private information to expose. That's a constituency that isn't often heard from and one that should be heard from."

CHAPTER 12

New Technologies

All the technologies we've considered have had one thing in common: They were developed to interact with something *addressable*.

Each device these technologies targeted had an Internet Protocol address that enabled the technologies to differentiate that device from other devices, assess the value of advertising to the person presumed to be operating that device, make a connection, involve the device in an auction conducted and concluded in an instant, serve an ad, or deliver the results of a search along with ads from advertisers paying to be associated with the search term. Our discussion of data in Chapter 10 was about assessing the advantages associated with a particular IP address, based on how that device's user browsed and responded before, and figuring out whether and when to present an ad to that address. All our privacy concerns arise because advertisers now have the ability to target a person and deliver an ad with pinpoint individuation to the person at his or her device's address.

Because it is addressable, digital advertising offers the ability to communicate with unprecedented specificity and finesse. Of course, a door-to-door salesperson presents products in an even more personal way. That's face-to-face selling. But that very personal selling often is coupled with little selectiveness about whom to sell to. The next customer of the door-to-door salesperson typically is the person who happens to live in the house next to the last house the salesperson visited. That's a roll of the dice insofar as targeting is concerned.

Online advertising has focused demographic and behavioral targeting with greater precision and put that fine focus together with instantaneous delivery. Even direct-mail marketing cannot do that. Using digital technologies, we now know the shopping habits and the interests of people who are using their devices behind closed doors in a way that a door-to-door salesperson couldn't know until the doorbell was answered and the salesperson was invited in and became acquainted with the people living inside. Today we know plenty about the behaviors of those users based on the web pages they go to and the links or ads they click on—without meeting them in person.

That might seem to some to be insidiously invading their privacy and hijacking their attention by means of their unique but leaky devices. But it also means that, over the long term, they'll be pestered less by irritating ads for products in which they haven't shown an interest. No business prospers if it wastes a lot of money advertising to the wrong people, no matter how cheap and efficient the advertising is.

That's a much bigger benefit than it at first appears, because the ways of presenting to consumers have become more numerous. For much of the development of online advertising, users were envisioned at home or work in front of a computer. But as the number and kinds of portable devices proliferated and their capabilities improved, that paradigm of the user perched in front of a single computer plugged into a wall socket has become almost as quaint and antiquated as the image of the door-to-door salesperson. The locations where we use our networked devices have expanded nearly worldwide. Addressability has never been so important. Like unmanned drones, ads are flown with a behavioral-targeting system for guidance.

As with search results and content, ads can be served everywhere. Randall Rothenberg, the CEO of the Interactive Advertising Bureau (IAB), acknowledged this ubiquity when, in announcing record 2012 digital advertising revenues, he wrote: "These record-breaking numbers represent a paradigm shift when it comes to marketers recognizing the role a multiplicity of screens plays in effectively reaching today's consumers."[1]

That phrase—"a multiplicity of screens"—suggests the diversity and influence of emerging technologies such as mobile telephony, tablets, and the adoption of apps that make use of HTML 5, as well as addressable TV. This final chapter sketches what makes each of them interesting and special and traces how the new technologies and new media channels are affecting advertising, behavior, and culture. In addition, for each of these new-media technologies, we will look at some businesses that have explored and exploited what these technologies make feasible.

The adoption of new technologies is frequently seen as disruptive, a displacing of predecessors. Yet all these emerging technologies owe an enormous debt to digital ad serving on the Internet. Digital technologies for targeting, search, and ad serving by real-time bidding have made possible the opportunistic, advantageous, and growing use of smartphones and tablets, apps, and addressable TV (as well as streaming video) for commerce as well as content. Online media, along with the advertising that has sustained them, have been the laboratory in which these new technologies have been spawned, endowed with their capabilities, and set on the path to being useful for business. The technologies for developing and commercializing digital media have sustained them in other channels for social as well as commercial purposes. That is one of the Internet's and the World Wide Web's enduring influences.

The Mobile Avalanche

The statistics pertaining to the spread of mobile in general and smartphones in particular have the rumble of an avalanche as it's beginning its descent. According to Visual.ly, an online marketplace for visual content, there are one billion active smartphones worldwide.[2] It has taken around sixteen years for the world to reach the first billion. It's forecast to reach two billion smartphones in three years.

Behind that momentum–gathering growth are two brute facts. The first is that you carry a smartphone on your person. It's always with you. That's inherently more valuable than something you have to make an appointment to use, like a PC that you don't always have at hand and that takes time to boot up. The second, according to Roger McNamee, a founder and managing director of Elevation Partners, a private equity firm in Menlo Park, California, is that "Children under the age of eight may never use a PC the way you do. An iPad or an iPhone is an eight–year–old's idea of a computer."[3]

These trends are particularly evident in the way we use social media. For example, of the roughly one billion users of Facebook, six hundred million typically use it on their phones. "As more phones become smartphones, it's just this massive opportunity," says Mark Zuckerberg, the founder and CEO of Facebook.[4]

According to the IAB, there are five main reasons for the surge in mobile advertising:[5]

1. The growth in device penetration

2. Faster transmission speeds

3. Improved display resolution

4. Increased sophistication in incorporating ads into mobile apps and websites

5. Shifting of social media consumption onto mobile devices

All these factors certainly are promoting the growth of mobile telephony. There is no question that smartphones are proliferating and are increasingly preferred over regular cell phones. The lines crossed in 2013 when worldwide sales of smartphones to consumers for the first time exceeded sales of regular cell phones (968 million smartphones vs. an estimated 838 million regular cell phones).[6] Smartphone unit sales grew by 42.3 percent compared to 2012, gaining a 53.6 percent share of the worldwide cell phone market.[7]

That growth in share had been expected for a number of reasons. Smartphones are increasingly serving as the go-to dashboard for users of different technologies. More than 30 percent of smartphone owners get apps and mobile Internet content a self-reported "several times a day."[8] Moreover, of the users who own smartphones, laptops, and tablets, 54 percent say they prefer their smartphone to the other devices.[9] Almost all (96 percent) of U.S. smartphone users who identify themselves as "smartphone content consumers" (103 million in 2012) download apps.[10] During 2012, the average number of apps downloaded was thirty-six.[11] Finally, of the users who owned a TV and a smartphone or tablet (the two-screen users), 84 percent spent an average of 1.7 hours using one of the devices while watching TV.[12] Of those who owned a TV, a PC, and a smartphone or tablet (the three-screen users), 64 percent spent 1.7 hours using their smartphone or tablet while using the TV or PC or both.[13]

"As smartphones get smarter, cellular networks get faster, and user penetration of smart mobile devices increases, the combination of personalization and location will have tremendous appeal to marketers. We are just at the tip of the iceberg," says David Silverman, a partner at PricewaterhouseCoopers.[14]

The Tablet Tsunami

Apple talks a lot about the "post-PC era," and it has made that more than a slogan ever since it began changing consumer behavior with tablets, most notably the iPad. Although Apple's tablet business lost share worldwide in

2013 to a group of manufacturers of tablets all using the Android operating system, Apple retained the lead among individual tablet manufacturers with a 36 percent market share (70.4 million iPads).[15] Its share was nearly double that of its closest individual competitor, Samsung (19.1 percent; 37.4 million Galaxy tablets).[16] Regardless of which company makes them, tablets are taking the spotlight away from PCs.

Around 44 percent of U.S. Internet users owned tablets by December 2013, a growth rate of roughly 6 percent compared to 2012.[17] Unit sales of tablets in the United States are forecast to grow by about 15 percent in 2014, to 89.3 million tablets.[18] Approximately 60 percent of tablet owners use it several times a day. The average usage amounts to fourteen hours a week.[19]

Although most tablet owners had been using PCs primarily, according to a report published in March 2011 by AdMob and Google, 43 percent of tablet users spend more time with their tablet than with their desktop PC and 77 percent said their desktop/laptop usage decreased after getting a tablet. One in three tablet users spends more time with their tablet than watching TV.[20] Those are the stark numbers of displacement.

"Tablets are one of the most rapidly adopted consumer technologies in history and are poised to fundamentally disrupt the way people engage with the digital world," says Mark Donovan, comScore's chief marketing officer.[21]

While smartphone users may use their phones more than tablets for on-the-go activities such as locating a store, checking a shopping list, or redeeming a mobile coupon, according to a Nielsen survey, tablet users are more likely to use their tablet for online shopping (42 percent of tablet users vs. 28 percent of smartphone users) or researching an item (66 percent vs. 61 percent) before buying it.[22]

"Once consumers get their hands on their first tablet, they are using them for any number of media habits including TV viewing," says comScore's Donovan. "Larger screen sizes [are] making tablets more conducive to video consumption than their smaller-screen-size cousins."[23] Tablet users are three times more likely to watch a video on their devices compared to smartphone owners, and about 10 percent watch video on their tablet daily.[24]

In 2012, almost all tablet owners (94 percent of Internet users, 70 million people) used them to access content: reading matter, news, weather reports, videos, and social media.[25] Increasingly, tablets are encouraging users to select their own mix of online programming.

Tablet owners show the same sort of serve–yourself attitude in their appetite for and selection of apps. The number of downloaders of apps for tablets went from 26 million in 2011 to 70 million in 2012. During 2012, 96 percent of tablet users downloaded an average of 22 apps.[26]

However, that average was affected greatly by a demographic trend. In the United States. the most voracious downloaders of apps for tablets were kids.[27] Of the apps downloaded to tablets in the United States in 2012, 45 percent were downloaded by children between the ages of 2 and 10. Clearly, one of the principal (although rarely acknowledged) uses of tablets in the United States is as a young child pacification appliance.

Although tablet app downloaders showed a three–to–one preference for free apps,[28] the money spent on apps almost doubled in 2012 in the United States compared to the year before, from $1.4 billion to $2.6 billion.[29]

When the Online Publishers Association (OPA) surveyed U.S. tablet owners about the business model they preferred for getting and using apps on their tablets, they offered survey respondents the following choices: (1) pay slightly more for an app with no ads, (2) pay slightly less for an app with some ads, and (3) get the app—with ads—for free. Over 50 percent of the survey respondents preferred to get the app for free even though it meant having to view ads when using it.[30]

Tablet owners who buy content for their tablets also tend to respond more favorably to ads.[31] They are more likely to research or buy a product after seeing an ad on their tablet than are tablet users who do not buy content for their tablets.[32] The average tablet user bought $359 worth of products from their tablets in 2012.[33]

According to eMarketer, the time U.S. adults spend with major media in 2014 by means of mobile devices has grown sevenfold since 2010 (24 minutes vs. 171 minutes).[34] An eMarketer forecast projects that, in 2014, U.S. adults will spend 23.3 percent of their time with major media by means of mobile devices, compared to 36.5 percent by means of TV, which has been falling slowly since 2010.[35] In addition, in 2014, for the first time U.S. adults are expected to spend more time engaging with major media by means of mobile devices (2 hours, 51 minutes per day) than by using laptops or PCs (2 hours, 12 minutes per day)—these stats do not include the time spent making mobile telephone calls.[36] As I write this in late July 2014, the lines are crossing in favor of mobile.

The net of all these trends is that mobile advertising is the fastest-growing ad format in the United States. It grew 110 percent in 2013[37] and has shown a compound annual growth rate of 123 percent since 2010.[38] Mobile is already more than the tail of the digital ad dog. Its $7.1 billion in 2013 U.S. ad sales is 17 percent of the total revenues for digital advertising.[39] Clearly, it's the fastest-moving part of the dog. By 2017, according to an eMarketer forecast, ads delivered by mobile devices will account for 64 percent of the total U.S. spending for digital advertising ($47.4 billion of a $74.1 billion digital total).[40]

That trend is already making things better for publishers who make the effort and investment to cater to tablet users. For example, at the Dive Into Media conference in February 2013, David Carey, the CEO of the magazine division of the Hearst Corporation, said that paid electronic subscriptions to Hearst's magazines had grown notably since the introduction of Apple's iPad Mini less than three months earlier, and that circulation for Hearst's digital editions had grown more than 12 percent in less than three months.[41] By June 2013, Hearst's digital subscriptions had grown more than 25 percent,[42] a maximal effect for the iPad Mini.

A number of other publishers are reporting similar benefits from the proliferation of tablet readership. According to a survey of fifty-eight magazines conducted by the Publishers Information Bureau, during the first quarter of 2013 ad sales for respondents' print editions showed virtually no growth compared to the first quarter of the year before.[43] They were just pedaling in place as if on a stationary bike. In contrast, sales of iPad ads for the same magazines grew by almost 24 percent during the same period.[44] The sales of ads for iPads were at least covering some new ground.

Ads for iPads accounted for 56 percent of all ad units sold by those fifty-eight magazines[45]—outselling print ads for those titles—and were the only reason those magazines' ad unit sales grew in the first quarter of 2013.[46] Almost the entire 7.5 percent growth in ad unit sales those magazines achieved in the first quarter of 2013 was attributable to sales of ad units to existing iPad users.[47] Those ad sales aren't surprising, in view of their owners' reading habits. As of June 2013, iPad users accounted for 84 percent of the web traffic going through tablets.[48]

[The iPad] "created an entirely new business model for publishing," says Gabriel Kahn, a professor at the USC Annenberg School of Journalism. "It allowed for deeper engagement and easier access to long-form content. Newspapers and other publishers finally found in the tablet the opportunity to introduce the paid-for app."[49]

Whether tablet users represent new subscribers (that is, an entirely new source of revenues) or previous subscribers getting content in a different way, the proliferation of tablets is evidence of a newfound-but-growing preference for another way of experiencing content.

Some view tablet usage as a repudiation of the ramified-and-wired-network model of the Internet, the use of computers and their browser programs as *the* way to get information. Respected tech investor Roger McNamee sees Apple's development of its app model for mobile content and commerce as, in effect, a bet against the World Wide Web. Certainly it's an alternative that offers significant differences. Apple's mobile operating system, iOS, is a proprietary system compared to the open-source Android system by Google. Apple's iOS offers not only a secure but also a very tightly controlled tech environment. It's a fundamentally different technology ecosystem, as compared to web browsing by means of computers. Says Roger McNamee:

iPads and iPhones are the most rapidly adopted, compelling, socially important products in a generation. The shocking thing was that Apple was able to charge $400 to $1,000 for devices that delivered a different experience of content that consumers were already getting for free over the World Wide Web. Apple sold huge numbers of iPhones and iPads, and became the most profitable company in mobile. Consumers paid Apple $400 to $1,000 to get away from the Web.

Even if the widespread adoption of mobile devices does not represent a consensus rejection of the PC–Internet model, large numbers of users have been captivated by apps and getting content on the bright, beaming screens of easy-to-carry smartphones and tablets. This isn't solely attributable to our attraction to shiny new toys. During the decade that led to the surge in adoption of mobile platforms, users were growing increasingly impatient with the wait-for-the-boot-up, computer-mediated, search and retrieve of the PC–Internet model.

The Changing Landscape

Mobile devices, with their versatile apps, are putting unprecedented pressure on the web-browsing model that has ruled for so long. Such mobile devices now account for over half of the connected devices in use worldwide, and they address a growing dissatisfaction with web browsing.

It is endemic to the PC–Internet experience that users stay on a page for a short time (and the time spent keeps getting shorter). The use of HTML 4 as the prevailing markup language for web pages, when combined with search engines, encourages users to scoot all over at lightning speed to get content. Get a link from the search engine results page; go quickly to wherever the link takes you. In a world in which everyone can search and in seconds find the nugget of information they want, and then move on, people have become used to hunting and gathering like restless nomads rather than behaving as patient, reflective farmers who stick around a web page. "Story-level engagement dropped dramatically as consumers navigated from page to page with increasing speed," says McNamee.

The fleeting use of online pages as cognitive stepping-stones has an erosive effect on commerce as well as on the comprehension of content. As engagement with editorial content diminishes, even less attention is paid to the ads, which, admittedly, often have not been masterpieces. Click-through rates have been plummeting steadily. "[Banner ads] are wallpaper," says Lewis D'Vorkin, the chief product officer at Forbes Media, a publisher that is in the business of selling media on which banner ads are presented.[50] Who remembers the wallpaper at a place you visited for less than 20 seconds?

This puts relentless downward pressure on the prices publishers can charge for their media, a worrisome result of the commoditization of online content.

Not only do these problems reduce publishers' revenues; they also focus attention on the limitations of the markup language used for the Internet: HTML 4. Why be concerned with the language the Web is written in? Those mobile devices, which are increasing in number faster than laptop computers are, need a better language to make the most of those apps. The use of HTML 4 has exhibited a number of limitations, all of which have made it disadvantageous for mobile.

Limits of HTML 4 and Their Effect on Mobile

The first of these limitations involves graphics. To include graphical elements on a web page in HTML 4, you have to incorporate proprietary Adobe Flash technology. Adobe Flash is written in a different code than the HTML 4 used on the other parts of the page. When combined with Flash elements, the data content of the entire web page could amount to more than a megabyte. To download such a web page could take more than a minute over a 3G cellular network, an intolerable delay to a cell phone customer. To make matters worse, downloading such pages could exhaust a user's data plan appallingly fast.

Second, because of the differences between HTML 4 and Flash, you can't search from the text into Flash or from Flash back into the text. This hampers the interaction of the editorial content and the ad copy. It diminishes how strongly they can be tied to one another.

Third, using Flash requires the page to be laid out in a rigid rectilinear grid, and it imposes severe limits on how much either the text or graphics, or both, can be modified. Putting a graphic using Flash on a web page is like embedding a brick into the text. Images are static objects that cannot be changed much. Everything is on one plane and locked in place. Not much can be done to adapt that graphic or the text around it.

Fourth, in the PC–Internet model, using HTML 4, every aspect of the page is laid out beforehand, resides on a server, and is delivered by a browser, as is. For example, when Condé Nast first published a digital version of *W* magazine, it was done as a PDF file. That has been typical for publishers; most of them publish PDF-based apps, which are customarily called *replica publications*.

Severe constraints are placed on how much the pages of these replicants can be revised. The PDFs are not scalable. Such pages are like tiny museum exhibits with technological security guards preventing you from touching the paintings.

Fifth, and finally, the typical web page usually has four Flash elements on it. These little islands of static content, whether ads or illustrations, compromise performance. The experience becomes less dynamic and adaptable. That might be okay if you just wish to view text, but it limits the usefulness of pages. To integrate video with HTML 4 is clunky. The depiction of full-motion video could appear unlifelike.

Effect of HTML 4 on Other User Experiences

"Desktop publishing platforms were not built with mobile [devices] in mind," says Dr. PJ Gurumohan, the cofounder and former CEO of GENWI, a company in Los Altos, California, whose technology enables cloud publishing for mobile. Clearly, the advent of mobile revealed the limitations of publishing by means of the PC–Internet model using HTML 4. It called for a different approach to publishing and commerce.

Mobile is different in three key ways. In the first place, it's tactile. You hold it in your hand. You execute commands by touching the screen. You feel it on your person. Second, mobile is contextual and reactive. It can take what you're doing into consideration. Whether you're driving. How fast you're moving and in what direction. It also takes into consideration which device you are using. Third, it is location sensitive. It can ascertain where you are and make use of your location. For example, whether you're near a particular store.

Because of this dynamism, mobile calls for a technology that can react, a technology that's responsive enough to change the content it's presenting based on how your experience may be changing. That brings us to HTML 5.

HTML 5 and Its Potential for Mobile

Although HTML 5 has not been officially adopted nor has it superseded HTML 4, it offers a variety of versatile new capabilities.

HTML 5 enables a publisher's or advertiser's content to be responsive to the mobile device being used. It can serve content based on the specific attributes/capabilities of the device on which the content is being viewed. It can rearrange the presentation to fit different devices.

HTML 5 empowers publishers or advertisers to store data locally. It can store the data needed for presentations on the mobile device rather than store the data somewhere on the Internet or in an online data storage facility. As a result, you can view the presentation when you are not connected to the Internet. Moreover, a publisher or advertiser can create an app that can run without an Internet connection. Very handy for something you carry everywhere. It can operate as if the "cloud" is in your pocket.

HTML 5 offers enhanced ability to take advantage of hardware acceleration. This allows smooth, realistic depiction of motion because of hardware animation, which enables you to do complex or interactive animations.

HTML 5 enables you to play video and audio without having to use a third-party proprietary technology such as Adobe Flash. If it's written with HTML 5, all the content is present in the app. You don't have to hunt elsewhere to get various aspects of the presentation. You can distribute the app by means of a browser, in which case the app would be called a *web app,* or you can distribute it by means of the Apple App Store or the Google Play Store. In either case, the app can run on a mobile device (as native to a mobile operating system) or in a browser (either Safari or Chrome).

With apps using HTML 5, content can be revised dynamically and disseminated with ease. This makes it cheap and easy for a publisher to provide readers with updates and new editions. Readers interested in a particular subject could be alerted to new developments by a publisher's editorial team or outside contributors and commentators—such as where to see new exhibitions of paintings by Vermeer. Easily updated sales literature sent to loyal shoppers of a store or catalog could tell them where to find sample sales or buy new limited-edition apparel at outlets in the same cities where the mobile devices are located.

Finally, with HTML 5 every pixel can serve as a programmable, responsive location. Every pixel can be used to enable readers to follow their interests by using the pixel as a link. Furthermore, every pixel can serve as the initiator of an app. This means that pixels used for a display ad can be programmed to enable a transaction. A user interested in buying what's being advertised can use the ad to make the purchase without having to leave the page.

The intelligence inherent in all the components written in HTML 5 enables the publisher or advertiser to present what you're interested in getting as if the pixels were little concierges. The content changes, but you can stay in the same place. Or you can move and the transaction processing capabilities can move with you. That puts an end to the searching, scurrying, and scrolling that are irritating with a PC and even more of a pain on a little handheld mobile device.

Publishing in the Cloud

GENWI (short for "generation wireless") is a start-up that has dedicated itself to enabling publishers and users to engage with content wirelessly, and using HTML 5 has been indispensable to its technology model. It coined the slogan "cloud publishing for mobile." GENWI has developed a cloud publishing technology that gives publishers the ability to create apps and publications in the cloud and then disseminate content from the cloud to any device or browser. A publisher can design and develop one app—say, for a periodical or retail catalog—which it can then disseminate everywhere.

One of the key differences of GENWI's system is that the design features of the publication reside in a separate layer in the cloud. The aspects of the design and variable details of the content are stored separately. Designs can be altered without affecting settled editorial content, and editorial content can be revised without altering design. "We de-coupled content and design in the cloud," says Gurumohan.

This allows publishers to develop apps and the publications that will make use of them in a novel way. They can manage content aggregation, build content models, and curate that content independently of having to worry about the design of the app. They can use—but they don't need to use—the Apple or Android store to distribute their app.

A number of other advantages derive from this cloud-based system. A publisher can get universal distribution for its app and, later, for the presentations offered by means of the app. The system also allows offline caching of the content. You don't need to be connected to use the content on your mobile device. The content can be revised by publishers in real time. And it can be personalized far more than it could be with HTML 4 because it can adapt to the preferences and locations of the individual user.

Building the apps with HTML 5 also offers ongoing flexibility to add various ad networks and native ads (content that appears to be journalism but has been paid for by an advertiser). Creating the publication layouts using HTML 5, and managing them separately, lets the publisher experiment with various ad networks and formats as the mobile ad industry evolves. Also, the ability to update content on the fly enables publishers to create content sections that are sponsored.

An open architecture for apps based on HTML 5 allows publishers to establish deep links with users, who may be reading editorial content or using search. Whether the content is being consumed by means of a native iOS app or a web app, for publishers it's akin to distributing a search engine optimization, or "SEO–able," magazine, as Gurumohan says.

In addition, there are a number of ways such a cloud–based system can save advertisers money in the areas of production and business processes.

Publishers new to digital publishing have tended to use a print–based work flow to develop their apps and content. That's understandable; it's what they are used to. But it can lead to enormous and needless expense. Many publishers still use print–type page layout tools to create interactive editions. However, when developing pages to disseminate to mobile devices, the number of page layouts increases enormously. Publishers have to adjust to different mobile devices that have different screen sizes, aspect ratios, and pixel densities, and those specs change all the time.

In addition to such costs of content production, many publishers incur excessive costs of customization. They have to develop systems to work with their subscription management platforms. They have to spend more to prepare full–page ads for different interactive formats. Finally, because the end product is digital, they incur additional costs to mesh their digital content with their company's analytics technology in order to develop stats, audit circulation, and so on.

Then, too, there are the costs associated with managing apps for publishers who are new to the game. Developing content so it can be presented by an app is the primary challenge, but there also are costs involved with managing and supporting a new app–distribution channel. Submitting apps to the Apple App Store is an exercise typically carried out by developers and programmers, the sort of personnel whom traditional publishers may not employ or may have few of. Then there are the costs of testing and debugging apps in development. In addition, there are the costs of supporting a digital readership that is getting acquainted with and increasing its expectations of digital publications and the personalization they can offer.

All these categories of costs are an outgrowth of grafting digital publishing onto a heretofore print-based publishing work flow, and they can mount up rapidly. They can be either eliminated or largely reduced by using a cloud-based system.

One standout example of the versatility that comes with such a cloud-based mobile content management system (mCMS) is that the platform enables in-app purchases by means of the Apple App Store or the Google Play Store. It also permits recurrent subscription payments. This allows publishers to offer payment arrangements that work as adaptably as the revision capabilities of the app-based publishing. For example, a publisher or a retailer could sell a book or a key feature of a book, magazine, or catalog using a subscription-pricing model. The payment arrangements can be one-off or iterative. This provides the same sort of flexibility about getting paid that the in-app publishing provides for revising the content. Because of the coordinated pricing and payment processing flexibility, new editorial products or services can automatically become new businesses and, in effect, brand extensions.

Digital TV

As with smartphones and tablets, most new media channels grow as their technologies are increasingly adopted, consumer by consumer. Not digital TV. The audience for digital TV expanded by government decree, on February 17, 2009, when all broadcasters ceased transmitting analog content over the air. On that date all U.S. TV viewers had to have digital-ready TVs or analog TVs with converter boxes to handle the digital signal, which became the only signal then permitted.

The audience for digital (and, in theory, interactive) TV has now grown to 115.6 million U.S. TV households inhabited by an estimated 294 million viewers ages 2 and older.[51] Numbers aside, marketers continue to regard TV as the most powerful branding medium in the world. "No other [medium] has the visual, auditory, and emotional engagement of TV," says Dave Morgan, the founder and CEO of Simulmedia, Inc., a TV ad–targeting firm and ad network. "Any other media impression is a poor substitute if you're trying to create a real impact on the potential customer."[52]

Marketers are voting that way with their wallets. In 2013, advertisers spent $74.5 billion for TV advertising (broadcast plus cable), a number that surpasses every other competing medium.[53]

But the rationale for the ad spending is getting shakier every year. Television remains the biggest (by dollars spent) advertising medium in the United States—if you add broadcast TV ad revenues to cable TV ad revenues. And there's no denying the size of TV's audience. But there is plenty of evidence that the audience is shrinking. For example, *the size of the TV-viewing population* (Americans ages 2 and older) *declined for each of the six consecutive quarters* from the third quarter of 2011 to the fourth quarter of 2012.[54] The total TV audience remains so large in part because Nielsen recently changed its definition of a TV household to include a subpopulation of households that it had not included before.[55]

Then there is the competition from digital media. In 2011, ad spending for all digital advertising surpassed ad spending for cable TV.[56] In 2013, ad spending for all digital advertising exceeded the ad spending for broadcast TV.[57]

So why is the ad spend for TV growing at all?

Viewers are watching more TV than ever: 4.28 hours per day, according to eMarketer.[58] TV is still where, in the aggregate, the most eyeballs are. In addition, there is a widespread belief among brand marketers that a mass audience is indispensable for gaining sway over the awareness process that leads to purchasing. According to Duncan Watts, a research scientist and social network theorist at Yahoo!, without audience exposure there can be no influence (sometimes called the *network effect*). "It is impossible to reliably generate large effects by targeting a few key influencers," says Watts.[59]

For these reasons, the ad spend for TV is growing. Brand marketers are choosing to place their biggest bets on the medium they view as having the best hope of effecting brand identification strong enough to move the needle.

Size isn't everything, however. Just because marketers continue to place so big a bet on TV, that doesn't make it correct. The question remains: Is that bet paying off? The answer to this question is cloudier.

The problem is audience fragmentation. In the past thirty years there has been an enormous increase in new media channels, not only outside of TV (computers, mobile phones, tablets, etc.) but also within TV. There has been approximately a sixfold increase in the number of TV channels and a hundredfold increase in the number of programs. In 1992, the average TV household was getting around 28 channels. In 2012, that rose to an average of 165 channels.[60] Even with a substantially bigger audience nowadays and record high total TV viewing hours per viewer, the content on those numerous additional and, often, special-interest channels has split today's big TV audience into so many more parts.

The ratings reflect that slicing and dicing. In 1993, three hundred TV programs had a 10+ rating. In 2013, only twelve shows had a 10+ rating. Half of all TV viewing is of shows with a rating of 1 or less. It isn't that so many of the shows are bad. Rather, the cratering of ratings is the result of the proliferation of choice. There are many more shows to choose among, with smaller audiences per show. The ratings are roughly proportional to the size of the audiences.

This splintering of the audience among so many channels has been particularly pernicious in prime time. In 1984, broadcast TV constituted 55 percent of all prime-time TV viewing. In 2011, broadcast content constituted only 30 percent of all prime-time viewing. The best shows the broadcast networks can offer—combined—don't draw even one-third of the viewing audience in prime time.

TV still has the biggest tent of all the circuses. But it's a tent with so many rings that you can watch only a few. Moreover, the number of viewers watching a particular ring is likely to be small, and shrinking. The usefulness for branding of those tiny tidbit audiences is open to question. Ratings have gotten so much lower (because audiences have become smaller) that it takes three times the number of ad impressions to reach one-third as many people.

This has given TV a "reach problem," says Dave Morgan. That is, with very few exceptions, shows are seen by fewer of the people that marketers want to target. "TV ad campaigns in the United States today deliver considerably less reach than they did in 1997 even though TV viewing is at an all-time high."[61] Yet, says Morgan, despite the diminishing returns, advertisers still bet the bulk of their budgets on a shrinking number of higher-rated shows. "The TV media industry has not adjusted its planning, buying, and measurement tools and strategies to keep pace," he says.[62]

> Fifteen years ago a heavy national schedule with average frequency would reach 80–90 percent of its target audience in three weeks. Today, most heavy multi-week national ad campaigns are lucky to reach 60 percent of TV viewers in their target audience.[63]

The situation is even worse when you realize how much more frequently the most-valued viewers are being bombarded by the same commercials today.

> Fifteen years ago, TV advertisers could expect 40 percent of their campaigns' impressions to be concentrated on the 20 percent of their audience who were the heaviest TV viewers. Today the frequency imbalance is almost twice as bad.... [T]hose 20 percent of

target viewers who are heavy TV viewers now receive 60 to 80 percent of most national TV campaign impressions. This squanders advertiser money, needlessly accelerates the "wear out" of creatives, and alienates target customers who feel bombarded by redundant messaging."[64]

Although TV media are still being bought in a way that appears to destine them to diminishing returns, the technology exists to make TV media much more effective and efficient for ad serving.

The major commercial advance offered by digital TV is the greater specificity it enables. Because of the data-gathering capabilities of digital TVs (or their set-top boxes), marketers can find out exactly what programming is being watched on individual sets on a second-by-second basis. This could be combined with lots of other usage information that may be collected and sold by cable TV system operators. As with the individual digital profiles that are compiled from the browsing and clicking behavior of Internet users, this expanding log of TV usage and viewing preferences can improve targeting markedly.

Advertisers can learn the demographics—for example, that a given household contains someone who is between the ages of 18 and 49. They can learn the finances: that a given household contains someone who watches a particular show, the household income is greater than $150,000 a year, and the household has investable assets. They can learn tune-in behavior combined with demographics—for example, that the household has a viewer between the ages of 18 and 49 who watched two episodes of *NCIS* this season. They can learn demographics combined with ad exposure: that the household contains someone between the ages of 18 and 49 who has seen eight ads for Oil of Olay since December 2013. Such information can be crunched by algorithms to create analytics to predict what programs those viewers will be watching and when.

Or forget the analytics. Just have the TV set tell advertisers in the moment what viewers are watching. Ping the set, and get the second-by-second viewing behavior as it happens. Then, as with real-time bidding for online advertising, buy the TV impression and send the appropriate commercial in a millisecond. Remember, *digital* TV is addressable. It has an IP address just like your PC or tablet.

The goal of such market research is to send an ad to exactly and only the individuals who will respond to it as the advertisers wish. Imagine three houses side-by-side in an upscale suburban development. It's the sort of nice neighborhood where, a hundred years ago, a traveling salesperson might have gone from door to door. Now no one needs to ring any doorbells, because the selling tool is already in the houses and the residents are mesmerized at the same time by the same program—let's say it's the high-rated show *The Big Bang Theory*.

To the forty-four-year-old guy in the first house, advertisers are sending a commercial for Budweiser. To the twenty-four-year-old woman in the second house, they are sending a commercial for Maybelline mascara. To the retired baby boomer in the third house, they are sending a commercial for a discreet home-delivery service for incontinence products. Same show, same commercial break. Different viewers, different commercials.

But what if the homes aren't side-by-side? What if they are all over America? What if the viewers are watching different programs, even low-rated ones? No problem. What if they are not watching broadcast TV? What if a desirable subpopulation of viewers is watching the American Heroes Channel on cable TV? No matter. Those same guys can get the beer commercial when the advertiser wishes. They are the pertinent prospects. They are all digital and addressable. They can all be reached in real time at the right time.

That's the *vision* of virtually perfect ad targeting on addressable digital TV. That's how targeting on digital TV would work if you could target TV viewers as well as you can target Internet users with online advertising. How realistic is that vision?

What addressable TV—with its splintered audience that is enormous in the aggregate—shows better than any other digital medium is the way the old paradigm represented by analog media has changed drastically. With analog media (TV, magazines, radio, newspapers), the attention of the audience was enormous in the aggregate, but what was scarce was the means of getting to it. To distribute print content you had to own printing presses and newsrooms. To distribute TV content you had to have broadcast licenses and TV stations. That took lots of money in the hands of a few people or organizations.

By contrast, in the digital media world, the ways of distributing content are numerous. What is scarce—or, perhaps it's better to say, small in scale—is attention when weighted by the far smaller numbers of viewers in those audience slivers. With digital content shown on PCs or tablets, a click-through rate of one user in a thousand is considered a good response. With the exploding number of choices of channels and the fragmentation of the TV audiences, what is scarce is getting the attention of enough of the right viewers in the moment or during a campaign that runs for a certain period. It's the extreme opposite of the engagement one can get by buying a 30-second spot during the Super Bowl.

That does not mean that digital TV has poor prospects. What makes online advertising work is the combination of data, targeting, addressability, and the ability to optimize. TV's notorious lack of interactivity, the laid-back, passive nature of TV viewing, doesn't have to be a barrier to exploiting it for targeted advertising, because now all of digital media's data, targeting, addressability, and potential for optimization can be used to make the advertising far more relevant for those slender, self-segmented clusters of viewers.

Because of the hyperfragmentation of the formerly mass TV audience, advertising by using digital TV represents the best example of buying an audience by culling individual viewers from under perhaps the world's longest—and steadily lengthening—tail. The question is: Is that approach being adopted? If so, is it working any better than the steadily less advantageous approach of buying a large TV audience the old-fashioned way?

The Future of Digital TV Advertising

Simulmedia has staked its corporate future on making that alternative approach feasible. If it does—or could—work, then Simulmedia would be a good spot to see all the pieces falling into place.

So is the new approach to digital TV being adopted? The answer is: not much.

Is the long-tail, digital optimization approach working any better? The answer is: yes, and, at times, much better, in the rare instances when it's adopted.

Earlier, we sketched the *vision* of unprecedented specificity by means of behavioral targeting in digital TV media buying and ad serving. The *reality* is that the technological means of addressing digital TVs nationwide is feasible, but the installed base of such TVs is way too small to make much difference.

Although broadcasters and cable system operators had to begin transmitting programming by digital signals in February 2009, few TVs have the internal circuitry or set-top boxes that could *send* as well as receive digital signals, and most TVs were not equipped with computer chips. The scarcity of such high-tech TVs has severely limited the addressability of the installed base of TVs for the purposes of ad serving.

The technology infrastructure nationwide does *not* allow ads to be changed at every TV household. Actually, the situation is far worse than that. Only about 20 million of the 115 million TV households have TVs that can receive individually targeted ads. Ten years ago, less than 1 percent of set-top boxes were digital. Five years ago, maybe 15 percent of set-top boxes, at most, were digital. Now around 40 to 50 percent of the set-top boxes are digital.

However, even that 40 to 50 percent figure is misleading. It encourages an overestimation about the reporting that could be gotten from the installed TV infrastructure in the United States. Around 50 percent of the digital set–top boxes deployed are the most primitive kind—what are called *2000-level* set–top boxes. They have so little memory that they barely have enough space to store the code necessary to execute instructions and log channel changes. They are not like a DVR. It's not as if they can crunch numbers and develop detailed data about usage in a household. Relatively few TV households have equipment that could provide feedback data (called *digital exhaust*) that could be used to characterize their users' viewing preferences.

What's necessary are sets that contain a computer and could be directly connected to the Internet, called *smart-connected TVs, Internet-enabled TVs,* or, simply, *IPTVs.* Such sets are, in effect, big tablet computers. With such TVs, advertisers would not even have to work with a broadcaster or cable system operator. They could change ads on those TVs over the Internet, just as they can now with web pages on PCs and tablets showing display ads.

The current situation is that America has 115 million households with the most powerful–for–branding media delivery device—the big TV screen with its engaging content—as well as the state–of–the–art reception technology—a Barcalounger at the optimal viewing angle—but not enough of the right high–tech plumbing to make the most of that immersive transmission medium.

There were few Internet–enabled TVs even two years ago. In February 2012, only 10.4 percent of all TV households had an IPTV. Now they are being sold in increasing numbers[65] and come equipped with services such as Netflix, Hulu, HBO+, and Amazon Prime. However, there is another infrastructure constraint. As of February 2012, only 47 percent of those TVs were connected to the Internet.[66, 67]

With online display advertising, however the impressions get sold, advertisers can do rifle–shot–precise targeting. Because of the low–grade infrastructure installed today, with TV there is so little targeting that we are just narrowing the spray of the shotgun blast a bit.

So how long before America's infrastructure of digital TVs becomes fully addressable at scale? It could take as long as seven years. That is how long it will take until the ads can be changed on really large numbers of individual TV sets. But the tipping point could come much sooner.

More important, as a practical matter, for the large numbers of marketing executives who have the ultimate responsibility to decide how to allocate gigantic ad budgets among different media, the changes will happen before most of them retire. Learning how to adapt to the advent of digital, addressable TV will be a career-preserving or career-eclipsing challenge they will not be able to avoid.

That doesn't mean that the ad serving and optimization being used for Internet advertising can't begin to be used on the installed base of U.S. TVs right now. It can. In the old days of nationwide broadcast TV, advertisers would spend a lot to buy a mass audience, and they would get a lot of viewers they wanted. They also would pay for a vast number of viewers they didn't want. The waste was massive. That sort of advertising was like a commercial fishing boat trolling a rich fishing ground with an enormous net. The net always brought up lots of fish they didn't want.

With fully addressable digital TV in the future, advertisers will pay for and get only the fish they want. And those fish will be jumping into the boat. No net necessary.

Now we're in a transition period. What we have now is what used to be a major fishing ground that is fragmented into ten thousand lakes, sort of like Minnesota, but with fewer fish in each lake. Experienced TV advertisers don't know how to work all those individual fishing holes. Yet, even though we can't target individual sets and change the ads being shown in real time and at will, it still is possible to use the data available to determine at which fishing spots large numbers of the desirable target customers are congregating.

A company like Simulmedia is using massive data, just as online advertisers or their demand-side platforms do, to decide which impressions to buy, to determine what combination of programs will give its clients' ads the most impact. "There's enough technological infrastructure [now] to do 400 percent better," says Dave Morgan.

Let's say an advertiser is aiming for an Hispanic audience. The intuitive ad buy would be on Spanish-speaking networks such as Univision or Telemundo. However, that doesn't mean that English-speaking programming wouldn't be a better alternative. In fact, according to Morgan, 82 percent of Hispanic TV viewing is on English-speaking TV. So, for an advertiser who is aiming at a Hispanic audience, Simulmedia crunches the data to find one thousand commercial spots for which Hispanics are 50 percent or more of the viewers. For example, the American Heroes Channel on cable has lots of Hispanic viewers. Buying spots on that channel may produce better results than on a Spanish-speaking network.

This is not putting together an audience from scratch, individual viewer by individual viewer, as can be done with online advertising. Nevertheless, it's an improvement. It is buying shrewdly selected TV impressions on programs for which the right sort of viewers are congregating in greater numbers.

TV networks need the same savvy media buying to promote their new programming. Unlike many brand advertisers, who load up on the few prime-time shows with big audiences, TV networks could not care less where their advertising spots run. Because their marketing is held strictly accountable for ratings results, they'll run their commercials for new series anywhere that gets them the sort of audience they want for a new show.

In one such recent engagement, Simulmedia worked with a major TV network on a promotional "tune-in" campaign to get an audience to watch the premiere of a new show in a competitive time slot. Rather than just buy a gigantic audience in prime time and keep its fingers crossed, Simulmedia analyzed the viewers of "surrogate shows" that the network thought would have the sort of viewers it wanted for its new series. Based on that analysis, Simulmedia's technology predicted which ad placements would reach high concentrations of the target audience and bought those commercials. With only 29 percent of the network's budget, Simulmedia bought over thirty million impressions on seventy-three TV networks. Those commercials got almost 460,000 viewers to sample the new show when it premiered. Simulmedia had gotten over 40 percent of the viewers of surrogate shows to watch the new show, a dramatically high response rate. That made Simulmedia's approach 27 percent more efficient (that is, at getting the right sort of viewers) than the other media–buying approaches used on the campaign combined.

In practice, however, using media most effectively is often not the only, or even the most important, criterion of merit in media buying. Factors other than the pace of the adoption of technology may drastically impact the effectiveness of TV advertising. Decision making in advertising often is influenced a great deal by contractual provisions that are customary in a given industry.

For example, the Coca–Cola Company sells its product, the Coca–Cola syrup, to more than 250 bottlers. Those bottlers expect the Coca–Cola Company to provide advertising support for the brand along with those zillions of gallons of syrup. Those bottlers, contractually, are guaranteed that the Coca–Cola Company will provide a certain amount of promotional media, which translates into a certain amount of gross ratings points. Media directors for Coca–Cola may be compensated for spending their budget to bring about a certain amount of media weight. They are contractually obligated to deploy a certain absolute tonnage of impressions, even if the effectiveness of those impressions is, perhaps, not optimal. Those Coke media directors may *not* be compensated for *fishing any better*—that is, purchasing impressions that work harder for the brand, ratings notwithstanding. Their incentive structure may be completely indifferent to what technology can do better.

Nevertheless, things are changing in TV advertising, and online technology is playing a role in an unexpected way, even though online media budgets are smaller than TV budgets. As the use of technology is making online ad buying more accountable, that, in turn, is forcing TV ad buyers to be more accountable. Social engineering can, at times, outweigh technological innovation.

Let's say a media director at a brand advertiser is in charge of buying online media (or of supervising the online ad buying at its agency). For those online ad buys, the media director can get incredibly detailed data about exactly who was targeted, what the ad buy cost, and what sort of response was achieved. This data is far more detailed than anything the TV media director typically can provide. Chief financial officers at brand advertisers, impressed by the data about online media, are asking TV media directors, "Why can't you make TV advertising work that well?" Such a question, from a CFO, is exacting because the TV ad budget is much bigger. So the need for justification is greater, and the answer, from the TV media director, has to be more convincing. If not, then the online media director has made the TV media director look bad. The last thing the TV media director wants to hear from the CFO is "Unless you can give me better numbers, I'm going to take money away from TV."

This scenario is happening every day, as online technology gains in power. Speaking of the TV media directors nowadays, says Dave Morgan, "Their world is a world of excuses."

Ultimately, such organizational psychodynamics may be more important than technology. But it has been the development of online ad technology, with its capacity for using data for great specificity in targeting and then optimization, that started the inexorable process that is disrupting TV advertising. Sooner rather than later, the impetus for using better targeting and analytics for TV advertising may come from those TV media directors who don't want their careers to be painted into a corner this way by competing colleagues.

Notes

Introduction

1. Of course, we pay for the devices we use to view content and we pay for Internet access service. What I am suggesting here is that, with very few exceptions, such as Dow Jones, which requires payment and has erected paywalls around its sites, we do not pay, as subscribers would, for the published content itself. That is paid for by the publishers, whether we choose to access it or not. For more on this topic, see Ari Rosenberg, "An Open Letter to the Open Letter Writers," *Online Publishing Insider*, May 16, 2013, http://www.mediapost.com/publications/article/200512/an-open-letter-to-the-open-letter-writers.html (accessed March 30, 2014).

2. Interactive Advertising Bureau, *IAB Internet Advertising Revenue Report/2013 full year results*, April 2014, p. 19, http://www.iab.net/media/file/IAB_Internet_Advertising_Revenue_Report_FY_2013.pdf (accessed April 27, 2014).

3. Ibid.

4. Ibid.

5. Ibid.

6. PricewaterhouseCoopers, *PwC Global Entertainment and Media Outlook: 2013–2017*, www.pwc.com/outlook (accessed April 27, 2013).

7. "U.S. Total Media Ad Spending, by Media, 2012–2017," *eMarketer*, March 2014, images at https://www.google.com/search?q=U.S.+Total+Media+Ad +Spending,+by+Media,+2012–2017 (accessed April 27, 2014).

8. "Total US Ad Spending to See Largest Increase since 2004, *eMarketer*, July 2014, www.emarketer.com/Article/Total–US–Ad–Spending–See–Largest–Increase– Since–2004/1010982 (accessed July 28, 2014). See the second table at that web page titled "US Total Media Ad Spending Share, by Media, 2012–2018, source: *eMarketer*, June 2014, table #174113.

9. Any search term. Suppose, for example, you search for the term "mountain bike." The web crawlers will find every web page on which that search term appears just as you typed it. In effect, they are creating a continually updated index of the entire Internet for that search term.

Chapter 1: The Congested Online Ecosystem

1. According to Wikipedia, between two and three million Ginsu knife sets were sold between 1978 and 1984. The knives were made, at least originally, in Fremont, Ohio. "Ginsu," *Wikipedia*, http://en.wikipedia.org/wiki/Ginsu (accessed March 23, 2014).

2. Most of us don't see white spaces because we have track records as online consumers; as a result, there is always some advertiser willing to bid enough to put an ad in front of us. But if you were a person with no track record as a consumer, or if you were someone who erased the cookies from your computer frequently, then you would see actual white spaces where the ads would ordinarily appear. Those white spaces are online publishers' nightmare: They are ad media that has gone unsold and, thus, are an opportunity gone forever.

3. Terence Kawaja, *Parsing the Mayhem: Developments in the Advertising Technology Landscape*, slide #13: "Carving Up the Stack—Network World," Keynote Address, Interactive Advertising Bureau Networks and Exchanges Conference, May 3, 2010. Kawaja confirmed that in 2014 intermediaries still receive approximately $3 of every $5 spent for ad media. A video of Kawaja's presentation can be found at http://www.slideshare.net/tkawaja/terence –kawajas–iab–networks–and–exchanges–keynote (accessed April 2, 2014).

Chapter 2: Search Engine Marketing

1. Borrell Associates, "Economics of Search Marketing," June 2009, p. 4.

2. Ibid., p. 6.

3. "US Digital Search and Display Ad Spending, 2012–2018," *eMarketer*, March 2014, report #169628, www.eMarketer.com/newsroom/index.php/category/press-releases/.

4. Nitasha Tiku, "The Problem with Paid Search," *Inc.com*, July 1, 2010, http://www.inc.com/staff-blog/the-problem-with-paid-search.html (accessed July 5, 2014).

5. Darren Dahl, "Small Players Seek an Alternative to the Expense of Pay-Per-Click," *The New York Times*, October 17, 2012, http://www.nytimes.com/2012/10/18/business/smallbusiness/as-pay-per-click-ad-costs-rise-small-businesses-search-for-alternatives.html?_r=0 (accessed April 23, 2014).

Chapter 3: Auctions and the Development of Paid-Search Advertising

1. Danny Sullivan, "The Google Decade: Search in Review, 2000 to 2009," *Search EngineLand.com*, February 1, 2010, http://searchengineland.com/the-google-decade-search-in-review-2000-to-2009-34830 (accessed June 28, 2014).

2. This and other direct quotations attributed to Bill Gross, as well as information relating to him, come from interviews with Gross.

3. Andrew Ellam and Marco Ottaviani, "Overture and Google: Internet Pay-Per-Click Advertising Auctions," London Business School, LBS reference CS-03-22, March 2003, http://www-scf.usc.edu/~csci572/papers/Overture.pdf (accessed June 28, 2014).

4. Ibid.

5. Ibid.

6. Danny Sullivan, "2001 in Review: Search Engine Marketing Gets Respect, As Does Search Generally," February 4, 2010, http://searchengineland.com/2001-in-review-search-engine-marketing-gets-respect-35174 (accessed June 28, 2014).

Chapter 4: The Google Eclipse

1. Because of certain technicalities, at times, some bidders would not be ranked.

2. "US Digital Search and Display Ad Spending, 2012–2018."

3. "OPEC," *Encyclopedia Britannica*, http://www.britannica.com/EBchecked/topic/ 454413/OPEC (accessed April 24, 2014).

4. "2013 Financial Tables" (unaudited for 2013), Google Investor Relations, http:// investor.google.com/financial/2013/tables.html (accessed April 24, 2014).

5. "US Digital Search and Display Ad Spending, 2012–2018."

6. Farhad Manjoo, "The Great Tech War of 2012: Why Google Will Win," *Fast Company*, November 2011, p. 114.

7. "US Digital Search and Display Ad Spending, 2012–2018."

8. "US Ad Spending: Online Outshines Other Media," *eMarketer*, November 2010, report #122072, www.eMarketer.com, p. 1.

9. John Frelinghuysen and Aditya Joshi, "Bain Brief: In Search of a Premium Alternative: An Action Plan for Online Brand Advertising," *Bain.com*, April 20, 2010, p. 1, http://www.bain.com/publications/articles/in-search-of-premium -alternative-an-action-plan-for-online-brand-advertising.aspx (accessed July 25, 2014).

10. Borrell Associates, p. 4.

11. "US Digital Search and Display Ad Spending, 2012–2018."

Chapter 5: Display Advertising and the Advent of Ad Networks

1. In the auto industry in the United States, for example, in forty-eight states either it is illegal or there are restrictions on an automaker selling a car directly to a customer. The very same act as when Apple sells you an iPad in the Apple store is a crime when "perpetrated" with a car by an auto manufacturer in those 48 states. James Surowiecki, "Shut Up and Deal," *The New Yorker*, April 21, 2014, p. 36.

2. According to one estimate, by Jonah Goodhart, the cofounder and CEO of Moat, an analytics company for online display ads, three hundred million new websites were created in 2011.

3. Joanna O'Connell and Michael Greene, "The Future of Digital Media Buying," Forrester Research, Inc., September 21, 2011, p. 2.

4. According to one estimate, by InternetLiveStats.com, there are over 949.1 million sites on the Internet, and the Internet will reach one billion websites by the end of 2014, www.internetlivestats.com/total-number-of-websites/ (accessed April 26, 2014).

5. O'Connell and Greene, p. 2.

Chapter 6: *Real-Time Bidding and the Transformation of Online Advertising*

1. Jo Bowman, "Real-Time Bidding—How It Works and How to Use It," WARC, February 2011, p. 2, http://www.improvedigital.com/en/wp-content/uploads/2011/09/Warc-RTB-Feb11.pdf (accessed April 10, 2014).

2. A wise man once wrote: "Don't fall in love with your media plan." Actually, it was Kevin Lee, the CEO of Didit.com, a search engine marketing consulting company, in Kevin Lee with Steve Baldwin, *The Eyes Have It* (Westport, CT: Easton Studio Press, 2007), p. 91.

3. Ibid., p. 122.

4. Ibid., p. 138.

5. "The Arrival of Real-Time Bidding and What It Means for Media Buyers," Google white paper, 2011, p. 6, http://www.google.com/url?sa=t&rct=j&q=&esrc=s&source=web&cd=1&ved=0CDYQFjAA&url=http%3A%2F%2Fwww.lemag.ma%2Ffile%2F124563%2F&ei=xbZnU9yoAZDnsASLsYLgAg&usg=AFQjCNEynG0nS8I1UsNx6G3o5FVP_vZAPA&sig2=2cbggNow-vfysF7_skKvnw&bvm=bv.65788261,d.cWc. (accessed July 25, 2014).

6. Bowman, p. 4.

7. "US Digital Display and Search Ad Spending Growth, 2012–2018," *eMarketer*, March 2014, www.emarketer.com.

8. Interactive Advertising Bureau, *IAB Internet Advertising Revenue Report/2012 full year results*, April 2013, p. 12, http://www.iab.net/media/file/IAB_Internet_Advertising_Revenue_Report_FY_2012_rev.pdf (accessed May 5, 2014).

9. "U.S. Real-Time Bidding (RTB) Digital Display Ad Spending, 2012–2018," *eMarketer*, June 2014, www.emarketer.com.

10. "U.S. Digital Search and Display Ad Spending, 2012–2018," *eMarketer*, March 2014," www.emarketer.com.

11. Ibid.

12. Ibid.

13. Ibid.

14. "US Real-Time Bidding (RTB) Digital Display Ad Spending, 2012–2018," *eMarketer*, June 2014; www.eMarketer.com.

Chapter 7: *How Real-Time Bidding Works*

1. Ramsey McGrory, "The Realities of Real-Time Bidding—What Publishers Should Know," *MyersBizNet*, December 15, 2010, www.mediabizbloggers.com/guest-mediabizbloggers/111851544.

2. I estimate that approximately one hundred billion cookies are placed on computers and other networked devices every day. My rule of thumb is ten cookies placed for every impression served.

Chapter 8: Right Media Builds Its Ad Server

1. Poindexter was named for the nerdy but brilliant nephew of the Professor, the nemesis of Felix the Cat.

2. In the discussion that follows, we repeatedly use click–through rate (CTR) as the metric. Many advertisers use it to determine the effectiveness of their ads. Other metrics that could be used include cost per acquisition (how many Internet users agree to sign up for whatever is being offered) or cost per lead (how many Internet users provide information and agree to be contacted by the advertiser). Such results are generally called *conversions*, and the metric pertaining to them is called the *conversion rate*.

3. Research in decision theory by psychologists such as Paul Meehl, Daniel Kahneman, and Robyn Dawes has shown that simple algorithms with factors all equally weighted often can predict outcomes better than more complex, multiple–regression algorithms or the intuitive predictions of experts. As Kahneman writes in *Thinking, Fast and Slow*, "A formula that combines these predictors with equal weights is likely to be just as accurate in predicting new cases as the multiple–regression formula that was optimal in the original sample. More recent research went further: formulas that assign equal weights to all predictors are often superior, because they are not affected by accidents of sampling." Daniel Kahneman, *Thinking, Fast and Slow*, (New York: Farrar, Straus and Giroux, 2011), p. 226.

4. Success is defined here as the ability to deliver an effective cost per click or cost per conversion (performance) as well as scale.

5. In a significant way, however, it was not a neutral, impartial system. The algorithm was still configured to buy impressions and fulfill campaigns *to maximize the revenues of the ad network*, Right Media.

Chapter 9: Real-Time Bidding in Action

1. Quoted in Stephanie Clifford, "Instant Ads Set the Pace on the Web," *The New York Times*, March 11, 2010, www.nytimes.com/2010/03/12/business/media/12adco.html?_r=2&emc=etal.

2. Jeff Green, "Cutting Through the Remarketing Clutter with RTB," *ClickZ*, April 27, 2011, http://www.clickz.com/clickz/column/2045970/cutting-remarketing-clutter-rtb (accessed June 25, 2014).

3. Ibid.

4. Ibid.

5. Mike Baker, "Real-Time Bidding: What It Is and Why It Matters," *ClickZ*, October 19, 2009.

6. Jo Bowman, "Real-time bidding—how it works and how to use it," WARC, February 2011, p. 4, http://www.improvedigital.com/en/wp-content/uploads/2011/09/Warc-RTB-Feb11.pdf (accessed July 25, 2014).

7. Bowman, p. 5.

8. Green.

9. David Kaplan, "MSNBC's Kim: Killing Pageviews Will Pay Off in the Long Term," *Gigaom.com*, October 7, 2010, gigaom.com/2010/10/07/419-msnbcs-kim-killing-pageviews-will-pay-off-in-the-long-term/ (accessed July 25, 2014).

10. Rajeev Goel, "Building Real-Time Bidding," *Adweek*, January 11, 2010, www.adweek.com/news/advertising-branding/building-real-time-bidding-101443.

11. "Reaction: MEA Digital's Ryan Sees Philosophical Challenge Ahead with Guaranteed Versus 'Best Ad' Placements," *AdExchanger*, April 25, 2011, http://www.adexchanger.com/ad-networks/mea-digital-ryan/ (accessed April 9, 2014).

12. Zach Coelius, "Why Real-Time Bidding Wins," *Ad Exchanger*, July 13, 2010, http://www.adexchanger.com/data-driven-thinking/why-rtb-wins/ (accessed June 25, 2014).

Chapter 10: The Impact of Data on Digital Advertising

1. J. Howard Beales III, "The Network Advertising Initiative: The Value of Behavioral Targeting," March 24, 2010, cited in "Data Management Platforms Demystified," white paper, Blue Kai, p. 5. The NAI report is available at http://www.networkadvertising.org/pdfs/Beales_NAI_Study.pdf (accessed April 28, 2014). Beale writes (p. 12): "[Behaviorally targeted conversion] rates are more than double run-of-network rates."

2. Paul Verna, "Top Digital Trends for 2012," *eMarketer*, December 2011, p. 12, http://www.scribd.com/doc/88047938/eMarketer-Top-Digital-Trends-2012 (accessed April 29, 2014).

3. Carla Rover, "Moat's Jonah Goodhart Continues His War on the Click," *The*

Makegood, January 31, 2012, p. 5, http://the-makegood.com/2012/01/31/moats
-jonah-goodhart-continues-his-war-on-the-click/ (accessed April 29, 2014).

4. Ibid.

Chapter 11: Data Collection and Its Effect on Privacy

1. About the Panopticon, Bentham wrote: "Morals reformed—health preserved—
industry invigorated instruction diffused—public burthens lightened—
Economy seated, as it were, upon a rock—the gordian knot of the Poor–Laws
are [sic] not cut, but untied—all by a simple idea in Architecture!" This guy
was way too enthralled by technology. Jeremy Bentham, quoted in *The Panopticon Writings*, ed. Miran Bozovic (London: Verso, 1995), Preface: www.ics
.uci.edu/~djp3/classes/2012_01_INF241/papers/PANOPTICON.pdf, p. 2 (accessed June 26, 2014).

2. Bentham, quoted in *The Panopticon Writings*, Preface: www.ics.uci.edu/~djp3/
classes/2012_01_INF241/papers/PANOPTICON.pdf, p. 2 (accessed June 26,
2014).

3. Federal Trade Commission, "Protecting Consumer Privacy in an Era of Rapid
Change," Preliminary Staff Report, December 2010, pp. i–ii.

4. According to comScore, 1.26 trillion banner ads were served in the United
States during the fourth quarter of 2013. There were ninety-one days in the
fourth quarter of 2013. Dividing 1.26 trillion by 91 yields 13.8 billion U.S.
banner ads per day. Assuming ten cookies placed for every banner ad, that
means 138 billion cookies placed every day.

5. The default setting on some browser programs (Safari, for example) does not
permit the placement of such cookies.

6. The purported privacy of our medical records is largely a sham. "Most phy-
sicians, patients, policy analysts, and journalists believe that the [Health Insurance Portability and Accountability Act (HIPAA)] 'privacy rule' protects
medical confidentiality. They are mostly incorrect.... [T]here is a belief that
the Department of Health and Human Services rules provide strong protec-
tions for medical information. Unfortunately, that belief is a misconception."
See Richard Sobel, "The HIPAA Paradox: The Privacy Rule That's Not," *Has-
tings Center Report* 37, no. 4 (July–August 2007), pp. 40–50.

7. Charles Duhigg, "How Companies Learn Your Secrets," *The New York Times
Magazine*, February 19, 2012, p. MM30, www.nytimes.com/2012/02/19/
magazine/shopping-habits.html (accessed April 29, 2014). See also the book

upon which the *New York Times* article was based: Charles Duhigg, *The Power of Habit* (New York: Random House, 2012).

8. Paul Ohm, "Broken Promises of Privacy: Responding to the Surprising Failure of Anonymization," 57 *UCLA Law Review* 1701 (2010), pp. 1719–1720.

9. Ibid., p. 1705.

10. Arvind Narayanan and Vitaly Shmatikov, "Robust De-Anonymization of Large Sparse Datasets," *Proceedings of the 2008 IEEE Symposium on Security and Privacy* 111, 121, Part I.B.1.c.

11. Ohm, p. 1721.

12. Ibid., p. 1704.

13. Nate Anderson, "Anonymized Data Really Isn't—And Here's Why Not," *Ars Technica*, September 8, 2009, http://arstechnica.com/tech-policy/2009/09/your-secrets-live-online-in-databases-of-ruin/ (accessed April 29, 2014).

14. *Edwards v. First American Corp.*, 610 F.3d 514 (9th Cir. 2010).

15. Electronic Privacy Information Center (EPIC), "*First American Financial Corp. v. Edwards*/Concerning Standing and Liquidated Damages for Federal Statutory Rights," p. 7, http://epic.org/amicus/first-american/.

16. Noah Feldman, "Strip-Search Case Reflects Death of American Privacy," *Bloomberg.com*, April 8, 2012, http://www.bloomberg.com/news/print/2012-04-08/strip-search-case-reflects-death-of-american-privacy.html.

17. Adam Lehman, "How Digital Marketers Will Survive the Coming 'Do-Not-Track' World," *Advertising Age*, June 21, 2012, http://adage.com/print/235528 (accessed April 29, 2014). Lehman is chief operating officer and president at Lotame.

18. Ibid.

19. "Report to the President: Big Data and Privacy: A Technological Perspective," President's Council of Advisors on Science and Technology, p. 38.

Chapter 12: New Technologies

1. Interactive Advertising Bureau, *IAB Internet Advertising Revenue Report/2012 full year results*, April 2013, Executive Summary, p. 4.

2. "Smartphone Users by the Numbers," *Visual.ly*, http://visual.ly/smart-phone-users-numbers (accessed April 21, 2014).

3. Roger McNamee, "How to Revive the Web," May 4, 2012, pp. 24, 26, http://www.elevation.com/downloads/Tech_Investing_10_Hypotheses_v8.6b.pdf (accessed June 9, 2014).

4. Brad Stone and Ashlee Vance, "Facebook's 'Next Billion': A Q&A with Mark Zuckerberg," *Businessweek*, October 4, 2012, www.businessweek.com/articles/2012-10-04/facebooks-next-billion-a-q-and-a-with-mark-zuckerberg (accessed April 29, 2014).

5. Interactive Advertising Bureau, *IAB Internet Advertising Revenue Report/2012 full year results*, April 2013, textbox headlined "The surge in mobile growth can be attributed to ...," p. 14.

6. "Gartner Says Annual Smartphone Sales Surpassed Sales of Feature Phones for the First Time in 2013," *Gartner, Inc.*, February. 13, 2014, http://www.gartner.com/newsroom/id/2665715 (accessed June 29, 2014).

7. Ibid.

8. Online Publishers Association, *A Portrait of Today's Smartphone User*, Slide 16: "At Least Half of Smartphone Users Access Content Daily via App and/or Mobile Web," August 2012, http://www.marketing.org/files/public/smartphone_study.pdf (accessed April 30, 2014).

9. Ibid., Slide 19: "Users with Multiple Mobile Devices Prefer Smartphones for Certain Uses/Content Types."

10. Ibid., Slide 22: "Nearly All Smartphone Users Download Apps: Averaging 36 Apps per User in Past Year."

11. Ibid.

12. Ibid., Slide 24: "Smartphone Users Show Strong Cross-Platform Tendencies: 64% on 3 Screens 1.7 Hrs/Day."

13. Ibid.

14. Interactive Advertising Bureau, *IAB Internet Advertising Revenue Report/2012 full year results*, Executive Summary, p. 4.

15. "Gartner Says Worldwide Tablet Sales Grew 68 Percent in 2013, with Android Capturing 62 Percent of the Market," *Gartner, Inc.*, March 3, 2014, www.gartner.com/document/2672716.

16. Ibid.

17. Consumer Electronics Association, "The Consumer Outlook on Tablets: Adoption, Sentiment and Social Media Conversation," January 2014.

18. Consumer Electronics Association, "U.S. Consumer Electronics Sales and Forecast," January 2014.

19. Online Publishers Association, *A Portrait of Today's Tablet User/Wave II*, Slide 5: "Tablets Have Become Embedded in People's Lives; 74 Percent Use Their Tablet Daily," and Slide 7: "Time Spent with Tablet Is High, Averaging 14

Hours per Week…," June 13, 2012, http://www.slideshare.net/victori98pt/ a-portrait-of-todays-tablet-user-wave-ii-june-2012-by-opa (accessed April 30, 2014).

20. "Understanding Tablet Device Users," *AdMob/Google U.S.*, March 2011, Slide 4, "Summary of the Tablet Study," www.gstatic.com/ads/research/en/2011_AdMobTablet_Study.pdf (accessed July 26, 2014).

21. Steven Musil, "U.S. Tablet Usage Hits 'Critical Mass,' comScore reports," *C|NET*, June 10, 2012.

22. "Mobile Devices Empower Today's Shoppers In-store and Online," Nielsen.com, December 4, 2012, www.nielsen.com/us/en/insights/news/2012/mobile-devices -empower-todays-shoppers-in-store-and-online.html (accessed July 26, 2014).

23. Musil.

24. Ibid.

25. Online Publishers Association, *A Portrait of Today's Tablet User/Wave II*, Slide 19: "Accessing Content/Information Remains the Dominant Tablet Activity and Is Increasing."

26. Ibid., Slide 30: "Appetite for Apps Remains Strong; Tablet Users Downloaded an Average of 22 Apps."

27. Ibid.

28. Ibid., Slide 36: "Tablet Users Increasingly Prefer Free Apps with Ads vs. Paid Apps."

29. Ibid., Slide 32: "72 Percent of App Downloaders Paid for Apps; Tablet App Market Has Almost Doubled."

30. Ibid., Slide 36: "Tablet Users Increasingly Prefer Free Apps with Ads vs. Paid Apps."

31. Ibid., Slide 38: "Tablet Ads Are More Impactful on Purchasers of Tablet Content."

32. Ibid., Slide 40: "Tablet Content Buyers Are More Likely to Purchase or Research After Seeing Ads."

33. Ibid., Slide 43: "Tablet Users Bought an Average $359 in Products from Tablets in Last 12 Months."

34. "Mobile Continues to Steal Share of US Adults' Daily Time Spent with Media," *eMarketer*, April 22, 2014, http://www.emarketer.com/Article/Mobile-Continues -Steal-Share-of-US-Adults-Daily-Time-Spent-with-Media/1010782 (accessed July 26, 2014).

35. Ibid.

36. Ibid.
37. Interactive Advertising Bureau, *IAB Internet Advertising Revenue Report/2013 full year results*, p. 4.
38. Ibid., p. 7.
39. Ibid., p. 13.
40. "US Total Media Ad Spending, by Media, 2011–2017," *eMarketer*, June 2014, Report #174136. Report is behind *eMarketer's* paywall; not available on the Internet. Must be requested from *eMarketer*, www.emarketer.com.
41. Gabriel Kahn, "Is Media Becoming Device Dependent?" *Mediashift*, column, June 7, 2013, www.pbs.org/mediashift/2013/06/is-media-becoming-device-dependent (accessed April 20, 2014).
42. Ibid.
43. Lauren Indvik, "Magazines Find Success Selling iPad Ads," *Mashable*, June 7, 2013, www.mashable.com/2013/06/07/magazines-ipad-ad-sales/ (accessed April 30, 2014); statistics: Publishers Information Bureau and Kantar Media, cited by the Association of Magazine Media; table of growth comparisons: *eMarketer.com*.
44. Indvik.
45. Ibid.
46. Ibid.
47. Ibid.
48. Mentioned by Apple CEO Tim Cook during the earnings call for Apple's third quarter of fiscal year 2013. His source: "June Tablet Update: iPad Usage Share Surpasses 84 percent," *Chitika Insights Report*, July 23, 2013, http://www.chitika.com/insights/2013/june-tablet-update (accessed April 30, 2014).
49. Kahn.
50. Lewis D'Vorkin, "Inside Forbes: It's Fight Night. PR Firms Take On Ad Agencies over Native Advertising," *Forbes.com*, July 22, 2013, http://www.forbes.com/sites/lewisdvorkin/2013/07/22/inside-forbes-its-fight-night-pr-firms-take-on-ad-agencies-over-native-advertising/ (accessed July 22, 2013).
51. "Nielsen Estimates 115.6 Million TV Homes in the U.S., Up 1.2 Percent," Nielsen Holdings N.V., May 7, 2013, www.nielsen.com/us/en/insights/news/2013/nielsen-estimates-115-6-million-tv-homes-in-the-u-s---up-1-2-.html. (accessed July 28, 2014).
52. Dave Morgan, "Sorry, the Internet Can't Fix TV's Reach Problem," *Advertis-*

ing Age, March 5, 2012, http://adage.com/article/digitalnext/internet-fix-tv-s-reach-problem/233110/ (accessed July 28, 2014).

53. Interactive Advertising Bureau, *IAB Internet Advertising Revenue Report/2013 full year results*, p. 19.

54. "Data Dive: U.S. TV Ad Spend and Influence (Updated—Q3 2013 Data)," December 23, 2013, www.marketingchartscom/television/data-dive-tv-ad-spend-and-influence-22524/ (accessed April 30, 2014).

55. Nielsen added households that get network TV programming for free over the air while getting other content by means of a broadband connection rather than from cable TV or satellite. While this is the smallest subpopulation of TV households, it has been the fastest growing. If this subpopulation had not been added by Nielsen in February 2013, then the number of TV households would have shrunk.

56. Interactive Advertising Bureau, "*IAB Internet Advertising Revenue Report/2013 full year results*," p. 19.

57. Ibid.

58. "Mobile Continues to Steal Share of US Adults' Daily Time Spent with Media."

59. Ibid.

60. Dave Morgan "TV Has a Growing Reach Problem," *Advertising Age*, February 28, 2012, http://adage.com/article/digitalnext/tv-put-mass-mass-media-anymore/232988/ (accessed July 28, 2014).

61. Morgan, "TV Has a Growing Reach Problem."

62. Ibid.

63. Ibid.

64. "... Sales of Internet TVs Have Been Taking Off Just in the Past Year," "Internet Disconnected TVs," *TechNewsDaily*, February 23, 2012, www.TechNewsDaily.com.

65. Ibid.

66. Andre Yoskowitz, "Report: Most Internet-Enabled TVs Remain Unconnected," *News by Afterdawn*, February 22, 2012, http://www.afterdawn.com/news/article.cfm/2012/02/23/report_most_internet-enabled_tvs_remain_unconnected (accessed April 30, 2014).

Index

About the Author

MIKE SMITH is Vice President of Revenue Platforms and Operations at Hearst Magazines Digital Media and General Manager of Core Audience at Hearst Corporation. The former President of Forbes.com and former Chief Digital Officer of Forbes Media, Smith is an authority on how using real-time bidding systems with finesse can dramatically promote online advertising and branding. Before joining Forbes, Smith was Vice President and Chief Information Officer at TheStreet.com. He also worked at HBO in a variety of positions, including Director of Information Technology. Smith is a graduate of the New Jersey Institute of Technology. He lives in New Jersey with his wife, Denise, and their children, Jessica and Michael.